SHRIMAD BHAGAVAD GITA AND MANAGEMENT CONCEPTS– MADE EASY

SHRIMAD BHAGAVAD GITA AND MANAGEMENT CONCEPTS— MADE EASY

**Useful for all people, especially the youth
Ladder for success**

DIWAKAR MISHRA
B.E. MBA

ZORBA BOOKS

Published by Zorba Books, June 2023
Website: www.zorbabooks.com
Email: info@zorbabooks.com

Title: **Shrimad Bhagavad Gita and
Management Concepts—Made Easy**
Author Name: Diwakar Mishra
Copyright © Diwakar Mishra
Artist: Adarsh Yadav (University of Allahabad)
Printbook ISBN :- 978-93-95217-75-0
Ebook ISBN :- 978-93-95217-76-7

The publisher under the guidance and direction of the author has published the contents in this book, and the publisher takes no responsibility for the contents, its accuracy, completeness, any inconsistencies, or the statements made. The contents of the book do not reflect the opinion of the publisher or the editor. The publisher and editor shall not be liable for any errors, omissions, or the reliability of the contents of the book.

Any perceived slight against any person/s, place or organization is purely unintentional.

Zorba Books Pvt. Ltd. (opc)
Sushant Arcade,
Next to Courtyard Marriot,
Sushant Lok 1, Gurgaon – 122009, India

DEDICATED TO MY PARENTS
AND WIFE CHITRA

PARENTS LAID A STRONG FOUNDATION,
AND CHITRA ACCOMPANIED ME IN
EVERY MOMENT IN LIFE

CONTENTS

BHAGAVAD GITA AS VIEWED BY WORLD FAMOUS PERSONALITIES

1. Albert Einstein (One of the most famous scientists in history):

"When I read the Bhagavad Gita and reflect about how God created this universe, everything else seems so superfluous." I have made the Bhagavad Gita as the main source of my inspiration and guide for the purpose of scientific investigations and formation of my theories.

2. Mahatma Gandhi (Father of the Nation):

"When doubts haunt me, when disappointments stare me in the face, and I see not one ray of hope on the horizon, I turn to Bhagavad Gita and find a verse to comfort me, and I immediately begin to smile in the midst of overwhelming sorrow. Those who mediate on the Gita will derive fresh joy and new meanings from it every day."

3. J. Robert Oppenheimer (American theoretical physicist known as the Father of the Atomic Bomb):

J. Robert Oppenheimer explains how he recited a line from Bhagavad Gita — "Now I am become Death, the destroyer of worlds." — upon witnessing the first nuclear explosion.

"We knew the world would not be the same," Oppenheimer remembered in 1965. "A few people laughed, a few people cried. Most people were silent. I remembered the line from the Hindu scripture, the *Bhagavad Gita*, Vishnu is trying to persuade the Prince that he should do his duty and, to impress him, takes on his multi-armed form and says, 'Now I am become Death, the destroyer of worlds.'"

4. Hermann Hesse (German novelist, poet, and the winner of Noble Prize in Literature in 1946):

"The marvel of Bhagavad Gita is its truly beautiful revelations of life's wisdom which enables philosophy to blossom into religion."

5. Carl Jung (Swiss Psychiatrist and Psychoanalyst):

"The idea that man is like unto an inverted tree seems to have been current in by gone ages. The link with Vedic conceptions is provided by Plato in his Timeous in which it states: 'Behold, we are not an earthly but heavenly plant.'" This correlation can be discerned by what Lord Krishna expresses in the chapter 15 of Bhagavad Gita.

6. E. Sreedharan (Technocrat and known as Metro Man of India):

"Many times I have faced the adverse situation. All problems I immediately drop it at the feet of the God. It gets immediately solved."

"Bhagavad Gita is the best management manual."

BLESSINGS

Everyone who is confused is Arjun. Arjun is the symbolic form of that state of the human mind when it becomes disoriented. Bhagavad Gita teaches us that whenever you reach a state of indecisiveness in life, you stand at the crossroads of thoughts, and your conscience is not supporting you as to which path to choose......? So then you go to the shelter of the Bhagavad Gita.

The Gita takes us out of every indecision and leads us towards the real and noble duty. Arjun said after taking refuge in the Gita that my delusion has been destroyed and I have regained my memory which makes me understand the path of my duty.

Shri Diwakar Mishra has prepared an essay on the subject of the book in a simple and lucid language, giving detailed examples for the first time in Hindi and English on Gita and Management. This book of Shri Mishra's "Gita Prabandhan" has become specially readable, memorable and collectable.

Dr. Shailendra Kumar Awasthi
(Advocate)

(Awarded with the "Raj Puraskar" by the President of the Government of India, Ministry of Law, "Govind Ballabh Pant" of the Ministry of Home Affairs, "Shiksha Puraskar" of the Ministry of Education, "Vidhi Bhushan" the highest honour of law literature of the Government of Uttar Pradesh, First Prize of the Human Rights Commission, prestigious award "Rajiv Gandhi National Knowledge Science Award "of Home Ministry.)

Tagore Town
Prayagraj

BLESSINGS

Shriyut Diwakar Mishra ji,

In the offered book, Shri Diwakar Mishra has explained in detail how Shrimad Bhagavad Gita can be implemented in practical life.

Ishwarah Paramah Krishnah Sachchidananda Vigraha |
Anadi Radirgovindah Sarv Karan Karanam ||

That is, Lord Krishna is the Truth and Bliss and He is the cause of all causes and He is Aadi, Anadi, and Govind.

Shri Diwakar Mishra has composed this book with the spirit of public welfare, in very simple words and pleasant manner; for this, thanks and best wishes to Mr. Mishra.

This book written with the wish of public welfare will be very much useful for all.

Sarve Bhavantu Sukhinah, Sarve Santu Niramayah |
Sarve Bhadrani Pashyantu, Ma Kashchid Dukha Bhag Bhavet ||

Devraj Pathak
Patron
Sanatan Ekta Mission, Prayagraj

GRATITUDE

I was born in Neemasarai, a small village in Pratapgarh district of Uttar Pradesh. My grandfather Pt. Shukdev Mishra was a renowned Shastri and a scholar of Vedas and Upanishads. My father Brahmachari Mishra was the youngest of six brothers. My mother Sharda Mishra belonged to a zamindar family of village Kharhar in Pratapgarh. My elder maternal grandfather (Late) Pt. Bhagwandeen Pandey was religious, kind, selfless, and a great soul. My maternal grandfather (Late) Shri Awadh Narayan Pandey, the youngest of three brothers, was a great devotee of Lord Shiva. I have always seen prayers, worships, and religious atmosphere in my maternal home, and it was from here that the seeds of spirituality were sown in my mind.

Soon my father brought us to Renukoot. My childhood was spent in the green valleys of Renukoot, a beautiful town surrounded by mountains. I studied here up to Intermediate. We used to go to the village during summer vacations. We had a joint family with many brothers and sisters. We used to play and have fun in the village. My elder uncle, tauji (Late) Shri Ramkumar Mishra was a visionary and saw far ahead of his time. He lit the candle of education in the family and inspired everyone to pursue higher education. The result is that today our family and children are working in high positions and settled in many metropolitan cities of the country. Many have settled in the US, Canada, and Australia. There are doctors, engineers, lawyers, chartered accountants, and factory owners in our family. Our family, children, and future generations will always be indebted to tauji Shri Ramkumar Mishra and will take his name with great respect and honor.

Shri Vijay Narayan Mishra, the eldest son of tauji and the eldest brother among us siblings, not only achieved higher education but also created new dimensions of success in life. He made the impossible possible in life. I followed him throughout my life and tried to move forward. His personality will always remain a source of inspiration not only for us but also for the generations to come.

I did my schooling from Hindalco School in Renukoot. It was here that my personality was formed. Our teachers not only taught us subjects but also taught us to be disciplined. They have taught us the values of life. Our Gurus Pandit Lakshmi Narayan Tripathi ji, Shri Shyam Shankar Dwivedi ji, (Late) Shri Shobhnath Pandey ji, (Late) Verma Behan ji, etc. have all shaped my life, gave wisdom, and taught us to keep courage in difficult times. Whatever position I have reached today and all my achievements are because of these teachers. I express my gratitude to all of them from the core of my heart.

Renukoot is famous for Hindalco Industries, an aluminium company established by the great industrialist Shriyut Ghanshyam Das Birla ji. Renukoot is situated near the Rihand Dam and is surrounded by the beautiful hills and valleys of the Vindhya Range. I grew up in the natural environment of Renukoot and in the loving company of the Hindalco family. I got the company of very good friends in my childhood, with whom I grew up playing. Friends Virendra Singh Baid, Shekhar Agarwal, Dinesh Jain, Rakesh Shukla, Akhil Sharma, Sunil Parwal, etc., the list is very long. All have filled colors in my life. Had they not been in my life, it would have been like a black-and-white art film. I am thankful to all my friends.

After successfully completing 36 years of service, I came home at Allahabad. Here I worked with some organizations and also taught in coaching centres. I did not have satisfaction and peace of mind. One day my daughter Rajshree asked me, what are you doing papa? I told her everything, and she told me that, papa, after retirement you should do that work for which you had a deep desire but could not do because of responsibilities and busy work life. After retirement, this is the time now you can take up and fulfil them. Do something noble for the society. I always had a special inclination toward the Bhagavad Gita. But it always seemed mysterious because it was difficult to understand. My daughter inspired me to write Bhagavad Gita in simple language for the common people and especially for the youth. I decided to write the Bhagavad Gita in simple language and bring out the hidden management concepts to surface, for the benefits of the youth. My daughter Rajshree and son Anant have contributed a lot in this writing work.

My father-in-law (Late) Pt. Onkar Nath Dwivedi was MLA from Pratapgarh and a highly respected personality. He was deeply religious and fond of spiritual books. I have used many texts from his collections in this writing. My mother-in-law (late) Mrs. Raj Dwivedi was a pious lady. She had deep knowledge of Ramayana, Puranas, and Bhagavatam. We used to discuss on various religious topics for hours. I am indebted to both of them for keeping my faith in spirituality more firm.

I am grateful to Shri Hari Mohan Sharma (alias Babbu) of Delhi. He is brother-in-law of my younger brother Dinesh. I have never seen such a selfless and pure-hearted person in my life. I have tried to learn a lot from his personality. I once again express my gratitude to him.

I am grateful to my friend Jyoti Mohan Srivastava (J M Srivastava) of Raebareli, who always supported me in life and encouraged in this writing work.

Inspired by daughter, I started writing about the Bhagavad Gita. I did not know the head or tail about how to write a book. At such a time, Dr. Shailendra Kumar Awasthi (Advocate), who is a constitution expert and a renowned author of more than 90 books on law, came forward to guide me. He suggested me the ways and means for this work and encouraged me. I started writing and it took almost two years to complete. I express my heartfelt gratitude to Dr. Shailendra Kumar Awasthi for his wholehearted support and constructive guidance.

The congratulatory message received from Shri Devraj Pathak, Patron of Sanatan Ekta Mission, Prayagraj, has made me spirited and overwhelmed. It is not possible for me to express my gratitude to him in words. I pray that his affection and support would continue throughout my life.

I am thankful to my family members who gave full support in my writing work. I am especially grateful to Rajshree and Ajay (daughter and son-in-law), Anant (son), Dinesh and Krittika (younger brother and his wife), Adit and Anagh (nephews), and Chitra (my wife), who encouraged and helped me in every way. Rajshree and Anant worked tirelessly on this work and produced research material to address difficult issues. Ajay designed the book and made special contributions on management topics.

I would like to thank all friends and well-wishers for their support in writing and publishing the book. With great pleasure and respect, I express my gratitude to all of you and hope that I will always get your affection, cooperation, and guidance like this.

Available literature, from the books composed by many great scholars, became the source of my writing; reference list of some of these treatises (granth) is given at the end of the book. Knowledge bank of books and lecture videos of world famous management expert and great motivational speakers Shiv Khera ji and Dr. Vivek Bindra ji were very useful in my writing. I am very much thankful to them. I express my gratitude to them from the core of my heart. The Gita upadesh of Ramanandsagar's Krishnavatar serial also became a source of knowledge. Ramanandsagar himself is a great Krishna devotee. I am especially grateful to him. I humbly express my gratitude to all these scholars, writers, philosophers, and motivational speakers. Many principles and forms of interpretation given in this book are based on these treasures of knowledge.

I hope this small book will prove useful to a common man, especially the youth, who are eager to know what is said in the Bhagavad Gita. With its knowledge, the mind remains disciplined, and doing selfless duty takes a man to the heights of success. In trouble, it strengthens the thinking process, instills courage, and shows the right way to move forward. It is an easy and simple means of achieving the purpose and goal of life. I have full faith that my effort will surely prove successful.

Diwakar Mishra
18-B, Tagore Town,
Prayagraj – 211002

PREFACE

There is a beautiful verse about Shrimad Bhagavad Gita.

Sarvoupnishado gavo dogdhaa gopal nandanaha |
Partho vatsah sudhirbhokta geetamritam mahat ||

All the Upanishads are like cows. The milk of knowledge that emerged from the udders of these cows is the Gita. Shri Krishna is the one who takes out this milk of knowledge. Arjun is like a calf, the one who gets this milk with the help of Shri Krishna.

Shrimad Bhagavad Gita is the Ganges of knowledge, devotion, and action, which has been flowing on this earth from centuries. The Bhagavad Gita was born in a very dramatic moment. This was the moment when the armies of Kauravas and Pandavas stood face to face for battle in Kurukshetra, and Arjun, the foremost warrior of Pandavas, refused to fight. Arjun was not a coward. He had fought thousands of battles, but in Kurukshetra, trapped in the mire of ignorance, affection, and attachment, he became indecisive. Arjun was in the same condition as a flamingo stuck in the mud. At this moment, Lord Krishna takes the command, and by the power of his inspiring teachings, raises Arjun from the state of despair to the state of clarity to achieve ultimate victory. The wonderful teachings by Lord Krishna converted Arjun from a point of low morale, deeply lost, restlessness, and cowardice to the level of high self-esteem, confidence, clear from all doubts and gloom, and fearless.

This is how the Bhagavad Gita originated. This knowledge, this philosophy is not only for Arjun but for all of us, for the entire human race. Because, like Arjun, there are moments in every person's life when it becomes difficult for him to decide what right path is and what his duty at that time is. The responsibilities and duties in the life of every living being is his Kurukshetra.

While we face the Kurukshetra of our life, on every step, like Arjun, we have to decide what to do and what not to do. Lord Krishna has provided the Bhagavad Gita to take the right decision when faced with these odd situations. With the help of the knowledge of Bhagavad Gita, man reaches the heights of success by conquering difficult situations.

The management concepts like leadership, decision making, vision, planning, communication, motivation, work ethics, organization culture and climate, man power handling, and so forth, are all neatly imbibed in the Bhagavad Gita. The western management thoughts deal with problems at material level, e.g., profit priority, considering work force as commodity, rat-race for career growth, rise fast and grow-rich-overnight culture, frequent hiring and firing, etc., which is all at external levels. The teachings of Bhagavad Gita tackle issues from grass root level of human thinking. Once the thinking process of a man is improved, it will automatically enhance the quality of his actions and results. The western thought of prosperity could not provide enough motivation to ensure betterment of individual life. Bhagavad Gita inspires and restores life through "Nishkam Karma," that is, by the process of selfless action.

Bhagavad Gita teaches the deep universal truth of life. It is a solution to all problems and a source of constant inspiration and knowledge for leadership. It is a comprehensive philosophical thought for all human kind. Researches, studies have proved that the teachings of Gita encompass all modern management principles and are relevant in today's world and the future to come. It has been highly recognized and adopted by many institutions and corporate world.

Although all 700 shlokas of Bhagavad Gita are gems of knowledge and wisdom. In the present study, I have selected, to my best knowledge, about 60 shlokas which contain management concepts and tried to explain them chapter-wise. I have endeavored to link shlokas to relevant management concepts. For the purpose of clarity and better understanding of the linkages, the basic concepts of management and the universal virtues of good leaders need to be revisited. Therefore, a brief write-up on core management techniques and virtues is given here below.

What is Management?

Management is a discipline. There are practitioners of this discipline, who practice management as a profession. As doctors practice medicine, and lawyers practice law, managers practice management. A manager's primary concern is the organization or the company with which he works. This is true regardless whether the manager works for a private or public sector or a multinational company; whether he is the executive director or the personnel manager reporting to the executive director. The professional manager always has his company's overall perspective in his mind; all his actions are guided by the company's objectives, and the most important — he is responsible for the performance.

A manager can be compared to the captain of a ship, who first has to set the course to reach the destination and then steer the ship along the course. Similarly, a manager, first of all, has to set the objectives which the firm must achieve. Objectives provide the direction in which the firm must move. Having decided upon the objectives, the manager must constantly monitor the progress and activities of the firm, to ensure that it is moving in the desired direction. This is the first and foremost task of every manager.

For actually performing all the tasks and discharge responsibilities, the manager must understand various systems and processes involved in managing. It does not matter whether you manage a private company, a public sector company, or even non-commercial organizations. The essentials of managing remain the same. Management process involves activities of 1. Planning, 2. Organizing, 3. Controlling and Directing, 4. Motivating and Leading, and 5. Decision making.

Universal Virtues of Good Leaders:

When we study and analyze outstanding leaders throughout history, who have made their mark by doing some lasting good to mankind, a nation, an organization, or a cause, we find that they come in all shapes and hues—the flamboyant, the scholarly, the artistic, the ascetic, the gregarious, and the recluse. And yet, when we look deeper into their personalities to find if there is something universal in their make-up, we really find that indeed that is so. Irrespective of the region of the world they belong to, and the era of history in which they had lived, effective leaders who leave a lasting impact after they are gone and continue to excrcise positive and inspiring influence on the minds of people have two things in common; both of these merit discussion.

Firstly it is possible to say that, in the totality of their personality, they were gentlemen in the true sense of the word. It is of interest to note that the definition of a gentleman and of "stihithaprajnya (स्थितप्रज्ञ)," that is, a man of steady wisdom as described in the Gita, is virtually the same.

Secondly, every outstanding leader has an inner hard core in him which is composed of certain universal virtues. If we piece these virtues together, then the integrated structure that emerges can be diagrammatically shown as in Fig. 1 and Fig. 2.

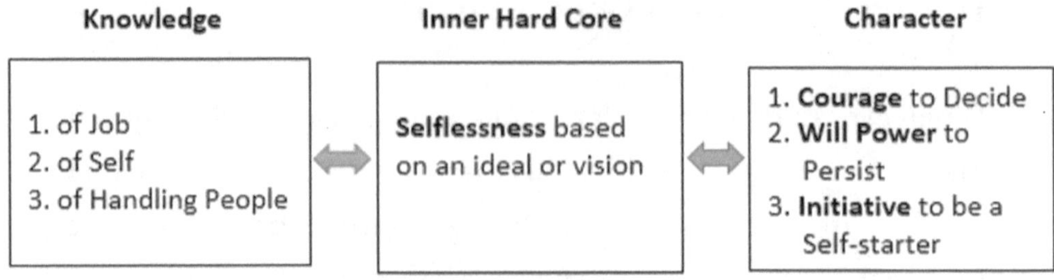

Fig-1. **Universal Inner Structures of Good Leaders**

Fig-2. **Selflessness Composition**

Reference: Strategic Management, Indira Gandhi
National Open University – 1991

SELFLESSNESS: Selflessness is the hub and heart, indeed the very foundation of this structure. Its two other components are knowledge and character. Knowledge helps a leader to determine "what to do" in a given situation. And the strength of character helps him "to get things done" by appropriately handling people who have to implement what he wants done.

It is essential to realize that selflessness is the fountain of all that is noble in human character, virtues without which it is impossible to influence others. Selfless man is neither greedy nor looking for shortcuts to get on in life; hence, his integrity never wavers. He seeks no unfair advantage over others; hence, sincerity and honesty come naturally to him. He is not a self-seeker; hence, his loyalty is steady and strong.

Selflessness is a relative virtue. Total selflessness is a rather rare phenomenon. When we look for examples of men who were completely selfless and lived for humanity at large, we spot Gautam Buddha, Jesus Christ, Prophet Mohammad, Guru Nanak, Ram Krishna Paramhans, Swami Vivekanand, Mahatma Gandhi, and the like. The most significant characteristic of these men is that they continue to have a tremendous impact on men's minds even after many centuries.

In the present context, we are just looking at leaders in normal organizations. Even at the working levels of small and big enterprises, some executives are more selfless than the others. For centuries it is reflected and appreciated that **the potential of effective leadership in an executive is directly proportional to the degree of his selflessness.**

CHARACTER: Each individual is a bundle of virtues and weakness, of mental and moral qualities. The resulting individuality of a person from this balance sheet is his character, or at times also referred to as his personality. The core qualities which are really important and which are invariably found in the character of all outstanding leaders are the following three: courage, will power, and initiative.

<u>Courage</u> — The most important fact of courage for a leader is to take decisions and to act.

<u>Will Power</u> — Will power to persist is another vital virtue

invariably present in all outstanding leaders. A good leader must have the will power (determination) to persist in spite of setbacks and obstacles that may arise in the implementation of his plan.

<u>Initiative</u> — An effective leader is always two jumps ahead of events. He does so by intelligent anticipation based on sound information system to overcome difficulties and obstacles that crop up. He is also on the lookout for openings and opportunities to exploit for the furtherance of his task. All these abilities are signs of initiative.

KNOWLEDGE: Knowledge is a major component of the universal inner structure of effective leaders, and has three sub divisions. The real secret of knowledge lies in what a leader learns through his efforts. A leader's direct experience in the field of work cannot truly be replaced by any other device; yet learning from other people's experience has been the very hallmark of all outstanding leaders. Learning is a lifelong and continuous process. The reading habit is the biggest single factor contributing toward indirect experience. History is the universal experience not of another but of many others.

<u>Knowledge of Job</u> — Knowledge of the field of one's work gives strength to a leader. The knowledge of the whole system and the internal and external environments of the organization is also necessary to get things done.

<u>Knowledge of Self</u> — A good leader must understand his own personality. This is absolutely vital. Leadership is the interaction between the leader and the led. An effective leader must know and understand both parties.

<u>Knowledge of Handling People</u> — How a leader handles people to get the best out of them is the essence of leadership.

In this act, the total personality of a leader comes into play. Handling people effectively needs understanding of two parameters — Human nature and Communication.

Krishnam Vande Jagatgurum

ARJUN VISHAD YOGA (PROBLEMS OF LIFE)

Preface:

This is a scene from the first day of the battle between the Kauravas and the Pandavas on the battlefield of Kurukshetra. The armies of both the Pandavas and the Kauravas are lined up opposite each other in an orderly manner. On the other side, in the palace, Dhritarashtra, the king, and Sanjay, his secretary, are engaged in a discussion regarding the battle. Sanjay has got divine vision by the grace of Maharishi Veda Vyasa, through which he is narrating a running commentary of the battlefield to Dhritarashtra, who was blind since birth.

Summary:

Dhritarashtra asked, "O Sanjay! My sons and the sons of Pandu have assembled with their armies on the battlefield of Kurukshetra, desiring to fight. What did they do then?"

Sanjay answered that Duryodhana observed the formation

of both the armies and went to Dronacharya to describe it. Duryodhana said that the army of Pandavas is adorned with great charioteers like Dhrishtadyumna, Satyaki, Virat, Dhrishtaketu, Yudhamanyu, Veer Uttamoja, son of Subhadra, son of Draupadi, etc. Here in his army, Dronacharya himself, Bhishma, Karna, Ashwatthama, Vikarna, etc. are decorated with great charioteers, and all of them are expert in battle. Bhishma is protecting his army, and Bhima is protecting the army of the Pandavas. Let everyone from my side protect Bhishma with determination.

Then, various instruments like conch shells, drums, mridang, narasinghe, etc. were sounded simultaneously from both the sides. That sound altogether produced by these instruments was fierce, echoing the sky and the earth. It was a custom in those days to give a warning about the beginning of a war.

At the same time, Arjun said to Shri Krishna, "O Lord! Please take my chariot between the two armies, so that I can see those who are eager to fight, and with whom I have to fight in this war."

On Arjun's saying so, Lord Krishna made the chariot stand between the two armies so that the opposing warriors, desirous of battle, could be seen clearly.

There, Arjun saw uncles, grandfathers, teachers, maternal uncles, brothers, sons, grandsons, friends, father-in-law, and well-wishers standing among the armies. Seeing all those relatives, Arjun's heart brimmed with emotions and compassion, and he said sadly, "Seeing my brothers and relatives present with the desire of battle, my body is trembling; I am getting nervous and horrified. My Gandeev (bow) is slipping from my hand, I cannot hold it any further, and I am completely bewildered by all this. O Keshav! I see bad omens coming. In this war, I do not see any good in killing my relatives. In order to regain this empire, for greed and its pleasures, I do not want to kill closest relatives, loved ones, and teachers. Even for the sake of the kingdoms of all the three worlds, O Krishna! I am not ready to kill them. By killing them, the family will be destroyed. When the family is destroyed, unrighteousness spreads in the whole family; women become depraved, and different castes mix. Due to the destruction of the family tradition, the souls of the ancestors fall down after being deprived of food and water. The moral structure of family and society collapses. With the destruction of family religion, disorder and anarchy will spread. The destruction of the family will be the cause of severe hell."

On the battlefield, grief-stricken Arjun was so filled with compassion and sadness that he, putting aside his bow and arrows, distraught, trembling, despondent, and terror-stricken, sat down on the chariot.

MANAGEMENT CONCEPTS:

Verse: 1.1

Verse: Dharmakshetre Kurukshetre Samveta Yuyutsavah |
Mamkah Pandavaschaiva Kim Kurvat Sanjay || 1 ||

Meaning: Dhritarashtra said - "O Sanjay! Tell me that in Dharmabhoomi Kurukshetra, gathered with the desire for battle, what did my sons and Pandu's sons do?"

By the grace of Veda Vyas, Sanjay was blessed with divine vision. That's why Sanjay was giving a running commentary to Dhritarashtra about the battle field. The crookedness of Dhritarashtra's mind comes to the fore in this verse. Instead of saying "what happened between our sons," he says that between mine and Pandu's sons, i.e., he created a separation. It is often seen in families and even in the corporate world that people talk separately in their respective groups. Every team, like marketing team, production team, sales team, etc., all have a challenge to meet the target. But instead of focusing on the larger objectives of the company, they remain confined to the small scope of their respective departments. This increases in-fighting among themselves and slows down the progress of the company.

The first quality of a true leader is to "Take the Ownership and Responsibility" of your team. Dhritarashtra, despite being the king of all, shied away from taking up this responsibility of ownership. The result was the terrible battle and bloodshed all round that could not be stopped.

Let us look at the first chapter of Bhagavad Gita in the context of management. In the first chapter, almost everything is spoken by Arjun. Arjun says — Krishna, I will not fight, I am nervous, trembling… I am completely bewildered. O Lord! Whatever you may say, I am not going to fight. Arjun was completely disappointed and discouraged. One notable thing is that in the entire first chapter, Lord Krishna did not utter a single word. Krishna wants Arjun to express completely whatever agony his mind is afflicted with. Whatever is going on in the heart and mind of Arjun, Krishna wants to know everything. Therefore, if He interrupts or speaks, the connectivity between Arjun and Him may break up. So, Lord Krishna, throughout the first chapter, remained calm and listened to Arjun.

Here we can see that, thousands of years ago, Lord Shri Krishna had given a wonderful management concept of "The Art of Listening."

Stephen R Covey, the world famous author on Management, has called it "SEEK FIRST TO UNDERSTAND, THEN TO BE UNDERSTOOD." In his famous book "The 7 Habits of Highly Effective People," this management principle is written in detail in habit number 5.

**"First Listen Carefully and Understand,
Then Narrate and Elucidate."**

Verse: 1.10

Verse: Aparyaatam Tadasmaakam Balam Bhishmaabhirakshitam. |
Paryaatpam Twidmeteshaam Balam Bheemaabhirakshitam || 10 ||

Meaning: Duryoadhan says, "This army of ours, which is being protected by Bhishma, is extremely powerful, whereas the army of Pandavas, which is being protected by Bhima, is very limited."

In this verse, Duryodhana is telling his guru (teacher) and army commander Dronacharya about the warriors of his army and their powers. Arrogance and pride are clearly visible in his words. He is unwittingly displaying his short-sightedness by describing the army of the enemy (Pandavas) as weak and less.

A true army leader never underestimates the power of the enemy. In the last moments of his life, Lanka king Ravana also taught a lesson to Lakshman: "Never consider your enemy as weak and small." Corporates in the industrial world also perform "SWOT Analysis" before launching a new product in the market. That is, the product is launched in the market only after studying it carefully from the point of view of its Strengths, Weaknesses, Opportunities, and Threats. They never underestimate the power of the market.

In this chapter, the way Arjun felt sad and nervous after seeing his brothers, gurus, and relatives on the opposite side, almost the same kind of confusion keeps appearing in front of managers in institutions. Sometimes, the manager is faced with two options, and one of them has to be chosen. One, either he has to do what is right and in the interest of the organization, or do what makes seniors or people happy. Under such circumstances, wrong decisions could be taken. Right and appropriate decisions should be taken for the health and progress of the organisation. Whether people are happy or annoyed, one should never succumb to emotions.

"Never Underestimate the Power of Your Enemy."

SANKHYA YOGA (THE ESSENCE OF BHAGAVAD GITA)

Preface:

Sankhya means knowledge of truth, i.e., the light of truth. The light that will illuminate the mind and dispel the darkness of ignorance forever. It means knowing, seeing, and understanding the Truth in reality as it is. In this chapter, Lord Krishna, condemning Arjun's delusion, cowardly frustration, and despair, encourages him to get up and go for the battle. Herein, mainly the duties and responsibilities of a man and **the knowledge of the truth of the soul** are described. This chapter is crucial because it contains the essence of the entire Bhagavad Gita.

Summary:

Lord Krishna says: O Arjun! From where did you get this fascination and this kind of cowardice at this critical time? This is disgraceful of you. Don't behave like an impotent, because it doesn't suit you. Abandon this petty weakness of mind and stand up.

After hearing such words from Madhusudan, Arjun says: O Krishna! How will I be able to shoot arrows at Bhishma and Drona in the battle? It is better to live by begging than to kill those who are respectable and revered by me. Hey Krishna! Emotions have undermined my personality; I have become weak, and my mind is distracted from duty. In this hour of crisis, I have come to your shelter, please guide me."

Thereafter, Lord Krishna guides the distraught Arjun by teaching him wisdom, action, devotion, and renunciation. Lord Krishna says: O Arjun! The soul resides within the body, but both are two different things. Soul is indestructible and immortal. It moves from one body to the other. Body is mortal. Body is made by nature so it moves according to the laws of nature. In this creation, one who takes birth is certainly subject to death. Every living being definitely has to die one day or the other; then the soul has to leave this body. So you are grieving for those (body) for whom you should not be grieving. Wise people do not mourn for the dead or the living (who are sure to die). There was never a time when I was not here, or you were not here, or all these kings were not here, and there will never be a time when we all will not be hereafter. The soul, in this body, passes from childhood to youth and then to old age, and after the death of the body, leaves it and assumes another body. He who thinks that he kills, and he who thinks that he is being killed, both do not know the truth. This soul neither dies nor is killed. It is lasting forever without end or beginning. It is eternal and perennial. It does not die even when the body is killed. Soul is a part of the Almighty.

Just as a man discards old clothes and dons new ones, similarly the soul discards the old body and dons a new physical body. Hey Partha! Neither any weapon can kill the soul nor can fire burn it. Water cannot drown it, and wind cannot dry it.

O Arjun! After knowing all this, you should neither mourn someone's death nor show the joy of killing someone. There is no greater duty for the Kshatriyas than to fight for the protection of Dharma (i.e., morals). That's why you do your duty without getting distracted. If you do not fight this war, you will fall from the fame of duty and will become a part of sin. People will always talk about your infamy, and for a man who has been respected, disgrace is worse than death. That's why O Arjun! Treat happiness and sorrow, profit and loss, victory and defeat equally and get ready for the battle. You will not incur sin even after killing them in the war.

O Partha! So far, I have told you the knowledge of Sankhya Yoga. Now I give you the knowledge of selfless Karma Yoga. This is an esoteric science. O Partha! One who understands its secret remains free from the bondage of the fruits of action, i.e., sin and virtue, while performing all actions of this world. One does not attract any sin. Any effort made through this path is not destroyed nor does any obstacle arise. Even a small part of this yoga makes a person fearless.

O Partha! Nishkama Karma Yoga says: You have only the right to act; you have absolutely no control over its result. The result of action or karma is a matter of future, and no one has seen the future, nor does anyone know. Then why worry in vain for something which is hidden in the future? Remember, the accomplishment of work (i.e., fruits) lies in the skill of doing the work, not in worrying about its result. Therefore, instead of dreaming of fruits while working, there should be feeling of happiness and fulfilment in doing the duty itself. Abandoning attachment to the fruits of action and keeping the mind equally composed in success or failure, go on doing your work with a sense of duty. <u>The balance of the mind in all situations makes a man a Karma Yogi.</u>

O Partha! Karma done without any desire is far better than the Karma done with the desire of getting fruits. Remember that a man cannot become Karma Yogi even after doing good deeds, if he has deep desires and lust for fruits for his actions (Karma). Intelligent people without longing for the fruits of their actions, composed in good or bad situations, continue to do their duty and climb the ladder of success.

O Arjun! Attachment is ignorance of the mind. Due to this ignorance man gets trapped in the temptation of worldly pleasures. He does not know that the body and all pleasures are mortal, illusory. When a man knows the difference between true and false or eternal and temporary, he becomes detached. He is not attached to anything. In other words, we can say that when the greed of attachment ends, man is not attracted toward anything in any way. He has complete control over his mind. When attachment is given up, this mind of man leads him to look into his soul, where he sees the divine. Because the soul is a part of the Almighty, i.e., God. When the mind is connected with the soul, the intellect becomes stable in every situation, good or bad. All the restlessness of the mind vanishes. The person who has attained this stage is called Sthithaprajna, which means keeping the mind even and steady without being distracted, in all situations of life like profit–loss, happiness–sorrow, success–failure, life–death, cold–heat, etc. That's why, O Partha! By removing the impurity of attachment from your intellect, try to see the divine by going into your inner self, become Sthithaprajna (composed wisdom) by practicing Karma Yoga.

After hearing such secret knowledge from the Lord, and after learning the method of unification with the God, i.e., Almighty, Arjun says: O Keshav! What kind of person is he whose intelligence is stable and whose existence is one with the soul? How does he speak? How does he live? And how does he work?

Lord Krishna explains in detail: O Partha! When a man gives up all the desires and lust, and when he looks into his inner self and experiences the vision of the Supreme Soul, he is called Sthithaprajna (person of composed wisdom). The mind of such a person is not disturbed by sorrow and does not take great delight in pleasure, and is free from attachment, separation, fear, and anger. Such a person, when faced with the lust of the senses, withdraws his senses from all sides, just as a tortoise in distress withdraws its limbs into its shell.

O Partha! One may turn away from the objects of the senses, but the lust for them still remains. The strong lustful senses forcefully disturb his mind. When a man runs after the wandering senses, it takes away his wisdom, just like the wind carries away a boat in the water. When a person's mind starts thinking about the lust of the senses, there comes about the affection or attachment for them. Desire arises from attachment, and unfulfilled desires lead to anger. Foolishness arises from anger, and memory is destroyed by foolishness. With the destruction of memory, the intellect is destroyed, and with the destruction of the intellect, the person itself is destroyed.

But O Partha! A person with a disciplined mind (equanimity), who controls his senses, enjoys objects without attachment, maintains the purity of his soul and incurs no sin.

O Partha! A man of composed wisdom (Sthitaprajna) is like an ocean. The water of the rivers keeps falling frantically, but the ocean remains calm. The power of the rivers is lost in its depths. The sea, however, never breaks its banks, and the water level inside remains the same. This is the position of a composed wise man. He does not get distracted by the continuous flow of desires. All kinds of lusts or pleasures are unable to create any kind of disorder and are lost in his mind. That is, a person with a stable mind does not have attachment to the senses even after enjoying all the pleasures, therefore he does not attract any sin. He enjoys the senses for his natural existence and not for any lust or greed.

MANAGEMENT CONCEPTS:

Verses: 2.2, 2.3 and 2.37

Verse: Kutastava Kashmalamidam Vishame Samupasthitam |
Anaryajushtamaswargayamkirtikaramarjun || 2 ||

Meaning: O Arjun! How did these thoughts enter your mind? How can you think of such useless things in these difficult times? This is not the thinking of an Arya (brave man). You will be disgraced and will never reach heaven.

Verse: Klabyam Ma Sm Gumah Partha Naitattvayyuppaddate. |
Chhudram HridayadaurbalyamTyaktottisthi Parantapah || 3 ||

Meaning: O Partha! Don't behave so impotent because it doesn't suit you. Abandon this petty weakness of mind, stand up, and go for the battle.

Verse: Hato Wa Prapsyasi Swargam Jitva Va Bojyase Mahim |
Tasmaduttishtha Kaunteya Yuddhaaya kritnischayah || 37 ||

Meaning: If you are killed in the battle, you will go to heaven, and if you win, you will enjoy the world. So stand up with determination and fight.

There are 18 chapters in the Bhagavad Gita. Arjun speaks in the first chapter. Lord Krishna has spoken in the remaining 17 chapters, and thus the knowledge of Bhagavad Gita has been passed on to humanity. In the first chapter, Lord Krishna only listened and understood Arjun, and in the remaining 17 chapters he narrated and explained the Truth of life.

In the first chapter, Arjun is completely discouraged and says, "My body is trembling; I am horrified; my Gandiva (bow) is slipping and falling down. O Krishna! I can't fight the battle." Hence the whole chapter passed in Arjun's grief. Arjun kept on speaking, and Krishna kept on listening.

From the second chapter onward, Lord Krishna begins to share the knowledge of the Bhagavad Gita with Arjun. Lord Krishna wants to bring about a change in Arjun. When a person is deeply dissatisfied, disappointed, full of cravings, and surrounded by ignorance, his knowledge, attitude, and behavior, i.e., complete thinking process, has to be changed in order to bring about change in him. Lord Krishna brings that change in Arjun by inculcating new value system with the teachings of Bhagavad Gita. Thus, Arjun was taken out of extreme despair and negativity to the heights of enthusiasm, determination, and positivity.

In the context of management, this is called "Managing Change." In the industrial sector, whenever the growth of the organization slows down, sometimes due to internal reasons and sometimes due to external reasons like technology obsolescence, search for new markets, etc. In such circumstances, corporates get the organization out of crisis by implementing the process of "Managing Change." The process of Managing Change is as follows:

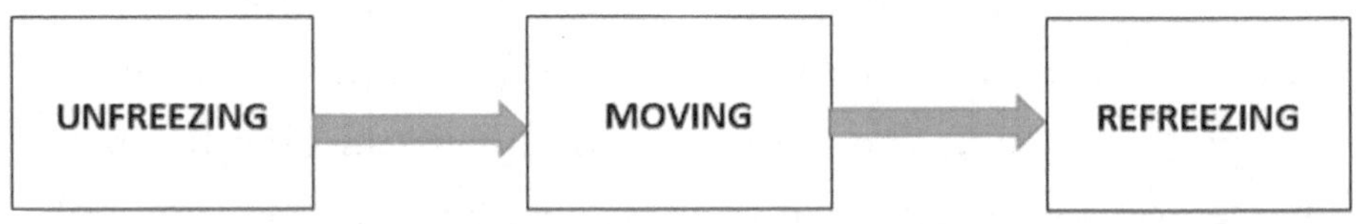

Managing Change Process

UNFREEZING

In practical terms Change does not occur on its own. It has to be brought about and implemented judiciously. People develop attachments to working in old ways and practices. They are accustomed to remain in the same status. New changes are not accepted quickly. To bring about a new change, first the emotions and the old knowledge base have to be loosened, melted. The fear of new changes has to be reduced in the minds of the employees. Informing them of internal problems and shortcomings, they have to be trained on the topics of need and benefits of new changes.

MOVING

This is the stage when the employees start believing in the New Change and are ready to accept it.

REFREEZING

This is the stage when new approach, new possibilities, and new plans are implemented in the organization.

Thousands of years ago, Lord Krishna presented a classic example of "Change Management" with the wisdom of Bhagavad Gita. From Chapter 2, Krishna starts speaking, and by Chapter 18, Arjun is completely transformed from weak, cowardly, and discouraged into a brave, determined, and spirited warrior.

THE KNOWLWDGE OF BHAGAVAD GITA IS AMAZING; IT HAS THE POWER TO TURN EVEN A MOUSE INTO A LION.

Verse: 2.7

Verse: Karpanyadoshopahatswabhavah
Prcchhami Tvam Dharmasamudhchetah |
Yachchreyah Syanishchitam Bruhitanme
Shishyasteham Shadhi Maam Tvam Prapannam || 7 ||

Meaning: Due to cowardice, my mind has become muddy. I have lost control. I am perplexed and confused. Tell me what

I should do in this odd situation. I am your disciple and have come under your shelter. Please show me the way.

In this verse, Arjun has completely surrendered before Lord Krishna, said that he has come to His refuge, and asked for His instructions and suggestions for the way forward. This verse is significant because here the follower (Arjun) has expressed his full faith and trust in the leader (Krishna), and is ready to take up the teachings.

One of the most important principles of management is "Effective Communication." Peter Drucker, the world famous author on Management, says, "The basis of a successful and good management system is the art of effective communication." If people or the employees do not understand it, how will they implement a good idea or process? The hallmark of successful communication is that connectivity should be created between the leader and the follower. Once there is connection, then it becomes easy to assure something. There are three levels of successful communication between the leader and follower.

Sr. No.	Stages	Importance
1.	Listen and Comprehend	50 %
2.	Build Connectivity	25 %
3.	Speak and Explain	25 %

Communication problems often occur in practical life, when there is no proper connectivity. If the salesman does not have proper rapport with his customer, then it becomes difficult to sell the goods. Between friends, within colleagues in offices, even between a husband and wife, if there is no proper connection then it becomes difficult to understand and explain. The first step in building a connection is to listen and understand.

In this verse, Arjun, while surrendering himself to Lord Krishna, asks the way forward. This is the stage when Arjun is completely united with Lord Krishna. Connectivity has been established between Lord Krishna (Leader) and Arjun (Follower). It has become easy for Lord Krishna to narrate, explain, and convince Arjun.

In this verse, Lord Krishna has presented a classic example of establishing "Effective Communication."

Verse: 2.14

Verse: Matrasparshastu Kaunteya Sheetoshnasukhdahkhadah |
Aagamapayinonityastamstitichhaswa Bharat || 14 ||

Meaning: O son of Kunti! Happiness and sorrow are like seasons of winter and summer, which come and go by. O scion of Baharat! They (happiness and sorrow) are born when the senses come in the contact with objects of lust, and do not last forever. Learn to bear with them without getting upset.

Good days definitely follow bad days in every person's life. In this verse, Lord Krishna has given the solution of "How to stay strong in difficult situations."

Lord Krishna says that change is the rule of nature. In this changing world, nothing lasts forever. Time always goes on. The seasons always keep changing. Today it is winter, tomorrow it will be summer. Similarly, good times also come with bad times in human life. Man gets entangled in troubles even without wanting to. Therefore, a man should understand that happiness and sorrow come and go by like the seasons. Difficult situations are not going to last forever. Change definitely comes. Accept the reality of difficult times and be patient. In difficult times, people often get scared and forget their goals. Instead of worrying about the past, think ahead. Therefore, accept the truth, let go of fear, focus on the goal, and start achieving it.

In all management books, leadership styles and qualities have been explained in detail. Almost all famous management authors have emphasized that a successful leader has strong will power. Backed by the strength of will power, he does not give up in difficult situations and is persistent in achieving the goal. Such people are a source of inspiration for the entire team.

Thousands of years ago in this verse, Lord Krishna has shown the way to keep the "will power strong."

**Tough Time Never Lasts, but Tough People Do.
Problems are Not Stop Lines; they are Guide Lines.**

- Robert H. Schuller

Verse: 2.41 and 2.44
Verse: Vyawsayatmika Buddhirekeh Kurunandan |
Bahushakha Hynantashcha Budhayovyawsayinam || 41 ||

Meaning: In Karma Yoga, the man has determined wisdom and singular goal. He remains firm in purpose. The intellect of those who are not determined, instead of being sceptical and focused, gets divided into many branches and strays away from the goal.

Verse: Bhogaishwaryaprasaktana and Pahritchetsam |
Vyawsayatmika Buddhih Samadhau Na Vidhiyate || 44 ||

Meaning: The intellect of those who live in luxury, comfort, and enjoyment ends soon. Their wisdom can neither hold fast nor stick to the goal.

Lord Krishna says: First decide your goal (occupation), then align yourself and your intelligence with that goal and go on toward achieving it. Many thoughts will come in your mind to divert your attention, but instead of wandering here and there, just focus on the goal, and you will definitely get success.

In this verse, Lord Krishna has explained the methods to achieve the goal. In the context of modern management, it is called MBO (Management by Objectives). Peter Drucker first started the concept of MBO in the industrial sector. Along with this, he pointed out the need to identify the Key Result Areas. There are some major action areas along the way in achieving the goal. Those areas need to be completed first before the goal is accomplished. These work areas are called Key Result Areas. Therefore, the first duty of a manager is to set a goal, then identify key result areas, and then focus working on the key result areas to accomplish the ultimate goal.

Lord Krishna says that in the way of achieving the goal, various thoughts encounter. Some are in the direction of the goal, and many are going to take you in different directions. In such a situation, a man should accept the thoughts which are conducive to achieving the goal and reject the thoughts which are inimical to the goal. By adopting this method, the goal is accomplished.

In the Mahabharata, there is a beautiful story about achieving the goal.

Arjun and the Bird's Eye:

Once, Guru Dronacharya decided to test all the disciples. He went to the forest with Pandavas and Kauravas and said, "Disciples! Today is the day of examination for all of you. Today is your test of how much you have learned so far in the archery taught by me." He made a wooden bird and put it on the tree and said to pierce its eye.

He first called Duryodhan and handed over the bow and arrow and said, "Vats! Aim and tell what you see." Duryodhana said, "Guruji, the bird is visible; the tree is visible; the sky is visible," etc. Dronacharya said, "Okay, you stand by the side," and called Yudihishthira and asked him to pick up the bow, aim and tell what is visible. Yudhishthira replied, "Gurudev, you, my brothers, this forest, trees, birds sitting on trees, leaves, etc. are visible." Dronacharya told him to stand by the side as well. After this, he called Bhima and handed over the bow and arrow. Then he asked Bhima what he saw. To this, Bhima replied that he could see Guru Dronacharya, his brothers, the tree, the mangoes hanging on the tree, everything. Dronacharya asked, "Is the bird's eye visible?" Bhima said that he could not see the bird at all. Dronacharya said, "Okay, you also go and stand by the side." In this way, Gurudev called Nakul and Sahdev one by one and asked them the same question while handing over the bow and arrow. Everyone said that they could see Gurudev, brothers, forest, earth, sky. Everyone was asked to stand by the side.

At last it was Arjun's turn. Gurudev called him forward, and handed over the bow and arrows to him. Then he asked Arjun, "Vats! Tell me, what do you see?" Arjun said, "I can see the eye of that bird, Gurudev." Gurudev asked, "What else do you see, Arjun?" Arjun said, "I cannot see anything except the eye of the bird." Guru Dronacharya smiled and said, "You are ready for this exam. Take aim, Vats." After getting the permission from the Guru, Arjun shot an arrow at the bird's eye, and the arrow went straight into its eye.

Krishna says: O Arjun! To achieve success, the focus should be only on your goal.

Living life without Goal is like playing football without a Goal Post. There is no purpose. Then why play the Game of Life? Therefore, you must have a Goal in Life.

Verse: 2.47

Verse: Karmanyevadhikaraste Ma Faleshu Kadachan |
Maa Karmfalheturbhuma Te Sangostwakatmani || 47 ||

Meaning: You have the right to do your Karma (duty), but you have no control over the fruits. You are not the creator of the results because it is not in your hands. You should never consider yourself to be the cause of the fruits of your actions, nor ever be indolent, and you must not be attached to not working.

This is a very popular verse. Yet due to lack of proper interpretation, it is sometimes misunderstood. This verse is generally taken to mean that Krishna says do your work, don't wish for the fruit. Krishna does not say so. He says **to focus your full attention on doing the work** and not on its fruits. If you focus only on the fruits, then your concentration will divert from the duty. How will there be results when there is no work toward them? Whatever action is taken is in the present tense, while its result is a future thing and remains hidden. When no one has seen the future, nor does anyone know, then why worry about it in vain? Remember, the accomplishment of work (i.e., fruit) is hidden in the ability and efficiency to do the work and not in worrying about its result. Therefore, work should be done for the sake of fulfilling the duty, not for the greed of getting the fruits. There are two ways to do any work. Either do it with worry or do it without worry. When a person works with worries, then different types of apprehensions surround the mind, such as "if I do this, will I get it or not?". Such type of worries gradually reduce the energy of man, and his capacity falls. That's why Krishna says **do your work without worry.** This is the secret of success.

In the modern management theories, there is a concept — "Work-Commitment." In this verse, Lord Krishna has explained what should be the right attitude and behavior for dedicated work-commitment. Work-commitment refers to the amount of enthusiasm in the mind of the employee to do his work. It is a sense of responsibility to get the job done efficiently. Lord Krishna explains that the **right attitude for work-commitment is the spirit of selfless action.** By working with this attitude, the employees become engaged and feel happy in the work.

This verse serves as an effective guide for working managers to conserve energy and prevent stress psychologically. It's a beautiful way to be happy and work effectively. Ego does not arise by acting selflessly. It also stops the wastage of energy due to the estimation of success and failure, profit and loss, etc.

"The Quality of Your Deeds Determine the Quality of Your Destiny."

Verse: 2.59

Verse: Vishya Vinivartante Niraharsya Dehinah |
Rasvarjam Rasopyasya Param Drishtava Nivartate || 59 ||

Meaning: The man may turn away from the objects of the senses, but the cravings for sensory enjoyments still remains in him. That craving goes away after darshan (seeing) of the God. It means when you experience a higher taste, it replaces the lower taste.

Before understanding this verse, let us listen to the story of Indra.

When Indra liked to be a pig:

Once upon a time, Indra, the king of heaven, disrespected his guru Brihaspati Muni. The Guru decided to teach him a lesson. He cursed him to live the life of a pig. Then Indra came to earth in the form of a pig and made his family here. Here Indra had a pig wife, had pig children, and many friends. He became the king of the pigs. He was very happy and satisfied with the life of the pig.

Meanwhile, the throne of heaven was vacant. Clouds of troubles began to hover over heaven. Seeing this situation of crisis, Brahma ji came to earth and said to Indra (who was in the form of a pig): "Bhadra! You have come on earth as a pig. Now I have come to save you. Come with me right away." Indra said, "Who are you?" Brahma said, "I am Brahma, don't you know? Come with me to your home, heaven." Indra said, "Brahma ji! What are you saying? I can't go with you. I have many responsibilities. I've got kids, a wife, and this beautiful pig society. I am very happy and satisfied. And you are advising me to leave all this comfort and go to heaven. I don't understand anything." Brahma said, "I have come to remind you that you are Indra, the king of heaven, not a pig. That's why, come with me." Indra said, "Lord Brahma! Are you serious? Will I get delicious food and environment full of filth like here in heaven? Will this family of mine be found there? I think, like an enemy, you have come with the intention of destroying my family."

Now Brahma was really confused. Indra was so satisfied in the life of a pig that he was even ready to give up the pleasure and splendors of heaven. Brahma with his divine power turned Indra back from a pig to a deity. After becoming a deity, Indra himself was surprised of what kind of a dirty pig's life he was living. He returned to heaven with Brahma and took up his responsibilities.

Lord Krishna says that there are three levels of happiness in life. Physical level, mental level, and spiritual level.

Spiritual Level of Happiness
Mental Level of Happiness
Physical Level of Happiness

Physical happiness is the lowest level; above that is the level of mental happiness, and at the top is spiritual happiness, which is the best. The vision of the God is called spiritual happiness. In this state, man attains the knowledge of truth.

Lord Krishna says that once a man gets a taste of the nectar of bodily pleasures, he becomes addicted to them. At the physical level senses are very strong and surround the man from all sides. He feels that this is everything and this is the whole world. He never wants to leave that stage. Relinquishing the lower level of happiness is possible only when the higher level of happiness is tasted.

This was what was happening with Indra. He was surrounded by the happiness of physical pleasures and became addicted to the same. He was not able to leave that stage.

Some people have such a belief that by reading the Bhagavad Gita, people leave their homes and become saints and start living in the forests. This is baseless and wrong notion. Nothing like this has ever been said in the Bhagavad Gita. Krishna says that you should not stop anything. All duties have to be followed and performed. All you have to do is cultivate and develop a taste for the happiness of a higher level. The basic desire of achieving the higher level of happiness remains hidden in all human beings. Hence, a man should try to reach up to the spiritual level by continuously developing a taste for the higher levels. There is permanent accomplishment.

In modern management, an important quality of successful leaders is "Handling People." For this, it is necessary to know the nature of human beings, only then they can be controlled effectively. In the field of psychology, there has been a lot of research on human nature. Out of these, "Maslow's Hierarchy of Needs" is the most popular and widely accepted. It is propounded by the American author Abraham Maslow. This is a psychological theory. This is known as the most important Theory of Motivation in psychology. All the needs are being called in a hierarchy because they can be fulfilled only in a sequential manner.

Self-Actualisation
Esteem Needs
Love and Belonging Needs
Safety Needs
Physiological Needs

Maslow's Hierarchy of Needs

Maslow's hierarchy of needs is a theory of motivation which states that five categories of human needs dictate an individual's behavior. The first need of man is physical satisfaction which is shown at the lowest level. Maslow has considered Self-Actualization to be the best and most important for a human being. That's why it is placed at the top. In self-actualization, a man gets the knowledge of the soul, that is, he recognizes the truth of life.

Lord Shri Krishna has explained in this verse that man should always develop the taste for needs of high levels. Maslow has shown this concept in his theory. According to Maslow, needs are met in a sequential manner. To fulfil these needs, man remains active throughout his life after being motivated and moves from lower to higher levels.

Verse: 2.70

Verse: Apuryamanamchalpratishtham
Samudramapah Pravishanti Yadvat |
Tadvatkama Yam Pravishanti Survey
Sa Shantimapnoti na Kamakami || 70 ||

Meaning: Just as the ocean remains unmoved even when it is filled with rivers entering it, similarly, the man in whom the pleasures of the world are pacified, he attains peace, rather than the man with desires.

Lord Krishna says that a man with a disciplined mind is like an ocean. Rivers continuously enter the sea. But there is no change in the water level of the sea. It remains calm and composed. Similarly, various desires and wishes will keep entering the mind of a man, but the goal will be achieved by the one who will not become lustful by being subjugated by desires. As the force of rivers merges into the depths of the ocean, so do all kinds of enjoyments into the mind of a disciplined man, unable to create disorders.

Story of the sage Vishwamitra:

The senses are very powerful. If the discipline in a man's mind is a little loose, then the man deviates from the goal. The great ascetic sage Vishwamitra was engrossed in intense penance in the forest for the creation of a new heaven. His penance was so austere and determined that he was completely oblivious to anything around him. Due to the penance of Vishwamitra, Indra, the king of heaven, felt his throne shaking. Then fearing his penance, Indra called Menaka, the nymph of heaven, and sent her to earth to break Vishwamitra's penance. Initially, there was no effect on Vishnamitra. But gradually he got attracted to Menaka and forgot his penance. Thus, his penance was dissolved.

In this verse, Lord Krishna has explained that if a man has to be successful in life and achieve his goal, then it is necessary to have strong will power inside him. A man with such strong will power has been compared to an ocean. In modern management, among the characteristics and qualities of successful leadership, a major quality—Strong Will Power—has been described. The great leaders of the world like Mahatma Gandhi, Franklin D. Roosevelt, Winston Churchill, etc., were all rich in strong will power and immense determination. With the help of this power, without being distracted from their goal, they have done great things for humanity at large.

Lord Ganesh is considered to be the most tolerant and patient deity. Whatever may be the circumstances, he does not lose his patience. He is the master of strong will power.

Let's listen to one of his story on strong will power.

Lord Ganesh wrote the story of Mahabharata:

Once, at the behest of Brahmaji, Maharishi Veda Vyas sat down to write the story of Mahabharata. He needed an intelligent person, the one who went on writing the story of Mahabharata spoken by him. He chose Ganeshji for this work. Ganeshji also agreed for this work but put a condition before Maharishi Veda Vyas that the writing of Mahabharata would have to be completed without stopping even for a moment. Ganeshji said, "If you stop even for a moment, I will stop writing." Maharishi

Veda Vyas and Lord Ganesh writing the Mahabharata

Veda Vyas accepted this condition, but Veda Vyas also put a condition before Ganesh and said, "Ganeshji, you have to understand first, then explain it and write." Lord Ganesh accepted his condition.

Veda Vyas started speaking the epic of Mahabharata orally, and Lord Ganesh started writing it quickly after understanding it. After writing for some time, suddenly Lord Ganesh's quill broke. Then, Lord Ganesh slowly broke one of his teeth, and dipping it in ink, continued writing the story of Mahabharata.

Maharishi Veda Vyas and Ganeshji took 3 years to write the epic Mahabharata. There are about 1, 10,000 verses in the whole Mahabharata.

Now let us listen to a short story on how ego destroys a man.

Clone:

A highly intelligent but arrogant man created ten clones of himself to deceive the Lord of Death. As expected, he escaped death twice as he could not be identified. On the third visit, the Lord of Death remarked, "You have created clones just like yourself but with one mistake." The man immediately stepped forward and angrily asked, "Tell me what's the mistake?" The Lord of Death said, "This is the mistake," and took him away.

KARMA YOGA
(WORK IS WORSHIP)

Preface:

In the previous chapter, Lord Krishna had only introduced Karma Yoga while explaining about Sankhya Yoga (or Jnana Yoga). In this chapter, the Lord has explained the necessity of Karma for survival, how to perform the prescribed Karma, the origin of Karma for performing Yajna as told by Brahma, the root cause of sin and its removal, etc.

Summary:

Arjun understood from Lord Krishna's words that knowledge is better than action. Hence, he asked the Lord: O Janardan! It seems from your words that Jnana Yoga is better than Karma Yoga, then why are you asking me to do evil deeds like war? Why are you inspiring me to kill? This is confusing my mind. Tell me clearly what is good for me?

Lord Krishna says: O Arjun! Long ago in this world, I

Preaching of Prajapati

preached two systems: The path of knowledge for contemplative persons and the path of action for active persons. Thus, Jnana Yoga and Karma Yoga are two different paths leading to the same city. The goal of both is the same — unification with God.

O Arjun! Undoubtedly, no human being can survive without working, even for a moment, at any time. That's why there is no freedom from working (karma) even if you remain indolent. Without work, even knowledge is not attained. Working is the rule of the universe. The person who keeps running only after enjoyment, lust, and luxury without doing the prescribed duty, he is called a fool and a hypocrite. O Arjun! It is better to control the senses of the mind and keep doing your duty without attachment. Without work, even your physical life cannot be sustained.

O Partha! When a living being is compelled to act, then he should act in such a way as a Yajna or welfare is performed. Yajna means labor done not for oneself but for others, for charity. Remember that all actions in this world, except those performed in the form of charity, are troublesome.

In ancient times, Brahma created Yajna along with creating living beings and informed living beings to perform charity, serve each other, and flourish. Being pleased with this service of yours, the Gods will give you the desired fruits. It should be understood that the person who eats food without doing charity is a thief. And those people who, after charity, enjoy food, they are freed from all sins. The life depends on food. Yajna brings rain, and Yajna is possible only through karma (action).

O Partha! This cycle of yajnartha-karma, that is, actions for the welfare of the people, created by Brahma, continues forever. This method maintains the order of the universe's existence.

That's why, O Arjun! Always do charity without being attached, then you will see the Almighty. Eminent people have to show examples of ideal actions to save others from unrighteousness and guide them onto the path of righteousness. The ideals they set, people start following them.

Hereinafter, the Lord explains about the work done by Himself: O Partha! For me in all the three worlds, there is no such thing that I cannot get, nor is there any work that is necessary for me to do, yet I am constantly engaged in work. Hey, Partha! If I stop working and become lazy, it will be very bad. Everyone will start following my path in every way, and chaos will spread in the society. People will start getting destroyed, and one day the whole world will be finished. That's why, O Bharat! The wise man should keep on doing ideal deeds to maintain the system of the world with the spirit of public welfare.

Lord Krishna encourages Arjun and tells him how to act without arrogance. He says: O Arjun! The man takes birth from nature. He keeps on working according to the qualities he has got from nature. By ignoring this truth, he becomes arrogant and thinks that he is doing all the work himself. That's why he has the full right to enjoy the fruits of the work. Nature has no contribution. Such people, living in the world of illusion, start running after the pleasures of the senses and thus walk toward the path of destruction. Therefore, O Arjun! Surrender all the fruits of your actions to me, and your ego will end, then fight valiantly without any desire.

Arjun asked: O Madhusudan! Under whose influence does a man commit sin? Often it seems that someone is forcefully pushing him toward sin.

Lord Krishna said: The things that push a man toward sin

are Lust and Anger. They arise from the mode of passion, i.e., Rajoguna. They are going to swallow everything, and are the great enemies of man. As a fire is covered by smoke, or a mirror is covered by dust, or a foetus is surrounded from all sides by the womb, so the soul is covered by the mode of passion. Desires arising in the mind and intellect through the senses act as the cover over them. Lust and anger cover the mind and intellect in such a way that the lamp of knowledge cannot be lit. Lust is fierce like fire, and by controlling the mind and intellect through the senses, overtakes man. Therefore, O Partha! First, deal with the senses, then conquer the mind, and then the intellect will be under your control. On the ladder of senses, mind, and intellect, the intellect is at the highest level. But the soul is superior even to the intellect. That's why, O Arjun! Recognize the form and power of the soul. And by illuminating the mind and intellect with this power, kill the formidable enemy of lust.

MANAGEMENT CONCEPTS:

Verse: 3.21

Verse: Yadyadacharati shresthastattdevetaro janah |
Sa yatpramanam kurute lokastadanuvartate || 21 ||

Meaning: Whatever a great man does, people start doing the same. The ideal he presents, people start following him.

In this verse, Lord Krishna has explained the conduct of a leader. Common people always need a leader who can educate them through practical conduct. People follow the ideals practiced by great people. People follow the leader who leads by example instead of only preaching. The way a leader behaves while performing the work and the example he sets, ordinary people start following him. It means conduct is the real personality of a leader. That's why the person who teaches and explains by his own conduct, leads by his own example, is called a true leader.

In modern management, one of the key principles of leadership is "Leading by Example." Lord Krishna has elaborated the knowledge of this principle thousands of years ago in this verse of Bhagavad Gita. This is a leadership style in which the leader first demonstrates the behavior he expects from his team members. He does not just push his team members toward excellence but actively participates and takes the entire team to the heights of excellence. It is a universal quality possessed by all the great heroes in history.

Leading by example gives people a reference point. They start seeing possibilities — thinking, "Look, if he did it, I can also do it."

To understand the reference point factor, let us look at the example of the 100 meter race in the Olympics. A person completed this race in 12.2 seconds in 1896. Since then, this record has been broken 13 times. In 1960, a person did it in 10.2 seconds. People wondered and started believing that if he could run in 10.2 seconds, they could do this even in less time. Carl Lewis did it in 9.92 seconds in 1988. Usain Bolt did it in 9.63 seconds in 2012.

"THE MOST POWERFUL LEADERSHIP TOOL YOU HAVE IS YOUR OWN PERSONAL EXAMPLE."
- John Wood

Verse: 3.27

Verse: Prakriteh Kriyamanani Gunauh Karmani Savanah |
Ahankarvimudhaatma Kartahamiti Manyate || 27 ||

Meaning: The man, deluded by the influence of the ego, considers himself to be the doer of all actions, whereas in reality all actions are performed by the three attributes (gunas) of nature. No work of nature is done alone. It can happen only by a combination and synthesis of different forces.

Lord Krishna says that all the work in the world is performed by natural forces together. Ignorant and egoistic man believes that he is doing everything. Such people live in illusion.

In this verse, Lord Krishna has explained the importance of "Team Synergy" and "Teamwork." Synergy is a cooperation that gives rise to a whole that is greater than the combination of its parts. It is true that no significant success is achieved by working in isolation. To be successful in big and important tasks, it is essential to know how to work in a group. Because man alone, on the strength of his limited power, cannot complete the work even in and extended period of time. Synergy and teamwork typically form when two individuals with different complementary skills collaborate. In modern industry, there is always a collaboration of people with organizational and technical skills. The success that is achieved by working collectively is not achieved by the efforts of any one person, but is the result of the joint efforts of the group. The success thus achieved is shared by all the members, and the happiness generated by the attainment of such a goal is multiplied.

A classic example of teamwork is a football team, which tries to win the game together, with mutual coordination. Another example is a Drummer, who uses four different rhythms to form a single drum-beat.

**ONE CAN'T WHISTLE A SYMPHONY ALONE,
IT TAKES THE WHOLE ORCHESTRA TO PLAY IT.**
- H.E. Luccock

**INDIVIDUALLY WE ARE ONE DROP,
TOGETHER WE ARE AN OCEAN.**
- Ryunosuke Satore

Verses: 3.36, 3.37, and 3.39
Verse: Ath Ken Prayuktoyam Papam Charati Purushah |
Anichchannapi Vaarshney Baladiv Niyojitah || 36 ||

Meaning: Arjun asked: O Krishna! Why is man induced to commit sin even when he does not want to? Who makes him commit this sin by force?

Verse: Kama Esh Krodh Esh rajogunasamudbhavah |
Mahashano Mahapappa Vddhyenmih Varinam || 37 ||

Meaning: Lord Krishna said: O Arjun! Those objects are lust and anger; they have arisen from the mode of passion or Rajoguna. They are going to swallow everything; their stomach is never filled. These are great sinners. Consider them as enemies in this world.

Verse: Avritam Gyanmeten Gyanino Nityavairina |
Kamrupen Kaunteya Dushpurenanlen Ch || 39 ||

~ 38 ~

Meaning: O Arjun! By this unquenchable fire of lust, which is the enemy of the wise man, the intellect of a man is clouded.

Lord Krishna is explaining in these verses that one should not draw conclusions based on imagination. If you do not understand anything, then you should ask. The subject should be clarified. Only then does the right thing happen.

Arjun was not able to understand some points in the Bhagavad Gita. He asks Krishna for more clarification: "O Krishna! I don't even have any desire, yet it seems that someone is forcing me to commit sin. Who is this making me commit sin?" The Lord explained: O Arjun! The desires within you increase even when they are fulfilled, and if not fulfilled, you become angry as to why they were not fulfilled. Thus, lust and anger are sinful. They are your enemies. Make you commit sins. Lord Krishna further clarifies: "O Arjun! These desires are like an unquenchable fire, which envelops your intellect from all sides. No matter how much you try to extinguish this fire, it flares up again."

One of the principles of the modern management is "Clarify Expectations." This principle is explained in this verse of the Bhagavad Gita. It means that, once a topic is clarified, a shared perspective and consensus is formed on the subject. By effectively clarifying the goals and ideas to the members, no misunderstandings arise during the execution of work, and mutual trust grows. When in the beginning of the task the expectations of all the members are made clear, then at the end of the task the team does not face any kind of disappointment. The attainment of the goal goes on smoothly.

In the industrial sector, situations like this often occur. Meetings are held regarding the progress of work in factories and institutions. In the meeting, discussion takes place with the managers of the concerned areas on the outline to meet the target ahead. After a certain interval, when the next meeting is held, the progress of most departments is found to be slow. That's when there are conflicts among the managers. The reason is that earlier meetings were concluded in a hurry, assuming "everyone has understood" without verifying whether "everyone has really understood". The result is not as expected. Therefore, at the end of every meeting, it is necessary to confirm and resolve all kinds of expectations and doubts of everyone. Only then the smooth progress is possible.

Verse: 3.40 and 3.41

Verse: Indriyaani Mano Buddhirasyadhishthanmuchyate |
Etairvimohayateesh Gyanamavrtya Dehinam || 40 ||

Meaning: O Arjun! The senses, the mind, and the intellect are the abodes of this lust. With the help of these three living places, lust clouds the wisdom of a man and keeps on misleading him.

Verse: Tasmatvamindriyanayadau niyamaya Bharatarshabha |
Pampanam Prajahi Hyenam Gyan Vigyannashanam || 41 ||

Meaning: That's why, O Arjun! You first control the senses and then with the help of prudence and wisdom, kill this great sinful enemy—"lust."

In the previous verses, it became very clear to Arjun that the enemy is lust. If you want to avoid sin, it becomes necessary to kill this enemy of lust. But he could not understand where does this enemy live and how to start killing it. He again requested

Lord Krishna for the clarification of all these points. In the verse 3.40, Krishna has described the living places of lust.

Lord Krishna says: The senses, the mind, and the intellect are the abodes of this lust. If lusts are to be eradicated, first of all, the senses, mind, and intellect have to be purified. If not done so, lust becomes so strong that it fascinates a man and clouds his wisdom from all sides. Then, man is unable to do anything and goes on sinking in the quagmire of sin.

When the existence of lust is known, how to start the process of destroying them? Krishna has explained its method in the verse 3.41.

Lord Shri Krishna says: O Arjun! For this, begin with the senses. First, it is necessary to control the senses. There are five senses: eyes, nose, ears, tongue, and skin (touch). These are the doors through which lust enters the human mind. To gain control, senses have to act according to the rules. Control the senses in such a way that you see only that, hear only that, smell only that, touch only that, and eat only that which is helpful in achieving your goal. Give up everything else.

A unique example of controlling senses is a dam built on a river. The dam first stops the flow of the river. Then according to the requirement, in a controlled manner, it keeps on releasing the water into the river. Similarly, a man should control the senses and use them judiciously. Always keep your mind dominant over your senses. Thus, gradually, a great evil enemy like lust can be destroyed. When pure material, i.e., noble thoughts and ideas, enters the mind through disciplined senses, the evils inside will be washed away. Thus, man can easily achieve the goal by climbing the stairs of success.

From the point of view of management, this verse is just an

extension of the principle of "Clarify Expectations." Arjun has asked Lord Krishna the solution to another curiosity related to desires. In the industrial sector, in institutions, this principle has great utility. It builds trust with everyone, with the customers, with the workers, and with the senior and junior managers. In today's management parlance, this is called "All Trust Behavior."

Stephen M. R. Covey has explained this principle in detail in his book "The Speedy Trust: One Thing That Changes Everything."

CLEAR IS KIND
UNCLEAR IS UNKIND

- Berne Brown

JNANA KARMA SANYASA YOGA (THE SECRET OF INCARNATIONS OF GOD)

Preface:

Jnana means knowledge of truth; Karma means Karma Yoga, and Sanyasa means the path of knowledge or Sankhya Yoga. Sankhya Yoga says that one should think like a saint, meaning that neither one should be attached to relationships nor should one mourn their breakup.

In this chapter, there is a special discussion on Karma Yoga from the third chapter. Herein, the secret of God's incarnations and different types of *yajnas* are described. For the complete success of Karma Yoga, there is a special description of the need and importance of knowledge.

Summary:

Lord Shri Krishna said to Arjun: O Partha! The selfless Karma Yoga that I have told you, I first told this yoga to the Sun in

God's Sermon to the Sun

ancient times. Partha! Sun passed this yoga to his son Manu, and Manu passed this to his son Ikshvaku. Thus received by tradition, this yoga was known to the sages. But after a long time, the yoga disappeared. Today, I have told you this ancient yoga. Because you are my devotee, and a friend too, I am telling you this secret knowledge.

Arjun said: O Keshav! You are born in this period, and Surya's birth is old, then how did you tell this yoga to Surya?

Shri Krishna said: O Arjun! You and I have had many births on this earth and will continue to do so in the future. The only difference is that you don't know this secret, and I know it all.

O Arjun! I am imperishable and unborn. I am the God of all terrestrial beings. Still, by subduing nature, I appear through my illusion, i.e., *yogmaya*. **Whenever righteousness and morals decline and unrighteousness rises, O Arjun! Then I take birth as an incarnation. To protect the virtuous, to destroy the wicked, and to re-establish righteousness, I appear in every era from time to time.**

One who thus truly knows my incarnations (divine-births) and deeds believes that unrighteousness will surely be annihilated. Such persons no longer deviate from the path of religion (morals) and ultimately unify with me.

A man gets what he does. Those who want the fruits of their actions soon here on the earth, worship the Gods who are nothing but different forms of Me, and perform sacrifices, because humans get the fruits of their actions in this world very quickly. O Partha! No one can live outside my rules. Although I am the creator of this material world, I am not considered as the doer of this action, because I do not desire or expect the fruits of this action. Even after creating the universe, I am detached from it, whereas the souls in the body remain bound in physical activities and the fruits of their actions. I only provide them with proper facilities and rules of nature's qualities to perform such actions. The soul itself is responsible for its deeds. A person who is aware of the nuances of this Law of Karma is not affected by the results of his actions. Understanding this truth and performing your duty without any desire for the fruits, i.e., selfless action, will definitely be rewarded with salvation.

O Partha! Let me tell you what karma, akarma (not in action), and vikarma (wrong actions) are. O Arjun! A person who acts with a selfless spirit does not have to suffer the consequences of that action, therefore his act becomes akarma. Karma is that action which is done with the desire for fruits; its fruit is necessarily received according to the action. The good for good deeds and the bad for bad deeds. Untruth, deceit, violence, etc. are wrong actions, i.e., vikarma. In wrong action, there are intense cravings for desires. A man who acts without the desire for the fruit, he, in other words, sees inaction in action. That's why one who works, abandoning the longing of desires, is said to have burnt his deeds in the fire of knowledge.

Explaining the characteristics of a Karma yogi, Lord Shri Krishna says: O Partha! Such a person's mind remains composed; he does not get involved in any materialism; he works only for the sustenance of the body and lives with equanimity in happiness and sorrow, success and failure, etc. When the attachment of such a Karma yogi is completely over, his mind enlightened by knowledge takes him inside his soul and lets him have the vision of The Divine. All the actions of such a person are dedicated to God.

Lord Krishna explains in detail about various types of Yajnas and offerings. Yajna is a ritual performed for welfare purposes. Lord says: O Partha! Dedicating any of your best things or any special feeling to me is called Yajna. The sacrifice of your dear thing is the basic spirit of Yajna. In other words, all this means 'give your best to the charity'. Yajna has been said to be of many types. Suppression of the senses is a kind of yajna in which all the actions of the senses are poured into the fire of self-control. Some people donate their material wealth, money, etc. That too is Yajna, called money-yajna. Many people donate knowledge selflessly. That is called knowledge-yajna. Many yogis engage in pranayama for spiritual attainments. For this purpose, by keeping a regular diet, by holding the breath they sacrifice the life in breaths. This is called prana-yajna, i.e., life-yajna. O Arjuna! Before doing this kind of spiritual practice, it is necessary to get instructions from an expert teacher.

Lord Shri Krishna says: O Arjun! Knowledge-sacrifice is much better than money-sacrifice. It means that the donation of knowledge is superior than the donation of money, because the supreme welfare of human can be achieved only by the power of knowledge. Knowledge is that fire in which all the faults, conceit, arrogance, etc. are consumed. Knowledge is the only way that makes man realize the existence and nature of God. When you have attained this wisdom, even if you are the biggest miscreant in the world, sitting in the boat of knowledge, you will reach across the ocean of sins.

Lord Shri Krishna says: O Dhananjay! We do not put the person in the bondage of life and death who has renounced the desires for the fruits of his actions through karma yoga, who has cut off all doubts through knowledge, and who has seen the divine in his soul. He gets salvation directly.

That's why O Bharat! Cut off all doubts in the heart arising out of ignorance with the sword of knowledge, become a Karma yogi, and stand up for the battle.

MANANGEMENT CONCEPTS:

Verse: 4.11

Verse: Ye Yatha mamprapadyante tanstathaiva bhajamyham |
Mam Vartmanuvartante Manushyah Partha Sarvashah || 11 ||

Meaning: I give fruits to those who take my shelter. Whatever may be, O Partha! People follow my path, live under my rule. Everyone follows my path in all respects.

Lord Krishna says: "O Arjun! The spirit with which man takes refuge in me, I give him the fruit accordingly." This means that no one can violate the divine rules. As he sows, so he reaps. As one does, so one pays. There is no exception in the divine law, that is, in the law of Karma. Everyone gets justice equally, that is, according to their ability.

Lord Krishna further says, "While doing some work, the kind of responsibility a person has in his mind, he gets the reward accordingly. That's why man should do his duty with full responsibility. If you take one step toward me, I will take two steps toward you. There would definitely be a reward, this is my assurance."

An important principle of leadership in modern management is "Ownership and Responsibility." This is the knowledge Lord Krishna has explained thousands of years ago in this verse of the Bhagavad Gita. Responsibility increases efficiency. Merely getting a post or position does not make one a master.

One becomes owner when he accepts the responsibility and accountability. Only then he is called a truly successful leader. Taking responsibility does two things: one is that the courage to take decisions increases, and secondly, the ability and capacity to solve problems increases.

To understand this, let us look at these two small incidents.

1. This is an old event. At a place in America, construction work was going on under the scorching sun. The workers were diligently engaged in completing the task. At the same time, a big car comes and stops. The glass of the window rolls down, and a voice calls from inside: "Come here, Steve." Steve was one of the workers. He looked up, and it was the voice of John, the company's Chief Executive Officer. Steve goes to the car. Both start talking jokingly. The car leaves after about five minutes. Steve gets back to work. He saw that his colleagues were surprised and curious. He then said that, few years back, he and John had joined the company together in the same position. The difference was that John worked for the company, and I for $28.

Let's look at another incident.

2. After retiring from the Indian Military Service, a colonel started his own business. Today, the net turnover of the company is about Rs. 1000 crores. One day, a friend of his came to him in search of a job. He asked, "Can I work with you?" Colonel said, "Why not? I have known you for the last thirty years." Friend joined the job. One day in the evening the friend and the colonel were talking. The friend said, "Look, both of us had joined the military service on the same day and in the same post as employees. And we retired together. And today, you are the owner, and I remained an employee. Isn't this a game of luck?"

Colonel said: When you are saying so, let me tell you an incident of 30 years ago. Thirty years ago, one day, after a hard day's work, both of us went to sleep in the barracks. We covered two miles on foot to reach the barracks. On reaching the barrack, I suddenly remembered that we had forgotten to switch off the lights and fan of the office. I told you this. Remember what did you say then? You said that after working hard from morning to night, we have reached the barrack by walking two miles. If you go to the office, you'll have to walk two miles and then you'll have to walk two more miles while coming back. Do you know what time it is? This time is 9.30 in the night. So, by the time we go there and come back, it will be 10.30. What is your problem, friend? It is only a matter of a light and fan. What's the big deal? There is only a light and a fan. Anyway, it belongs to the government. Whatever you say, I am not going there. And saying this you went to sleep. I went to the office alone, switched off the lights and fan, came back to the barrack, and then went to sleep. Now listen carefully to what I am going to tell you. You and I joined the army on the same day, okay. You used to get 1000 rupees; I also used to get 1000 rupees. That is also fine. You said that you were an employee before and are still an employee today. That's fine too. But that night I was the owner, and you were the employee, so even today I am the owner and you are the employee.

**"One becomes Owner only after
accepting Responsibility and Accountability."**

Verse: 4.13

Verse: Chaturvarnyam Maya Srishtam Gunkarmavibhagashah |
Tasya Kartaramapi Maam Vidhayakartamavyayam || 13 ||

Meaning: I have created four divisions of human society according to the three virtues and deeds of nature. Even then you should consider me to be the non-doer and imperishable. I do not do any work or intervene or change anything into that working system.

Lord Krishna says: In the creation of the universe, while creating human beings, I divided them into four divisions according to nature-born qualities (Satogun, Rajogun, Tamogun) and deeds. The meaning of this creation is that according to his department, man should do that work in which he is proficient. When the right person is engaged in the right work, harmony prevails in the society. Society continues to progress.

Here the meaning of virtue is psychological, that is, mental power. Man's inclination is formed according to thinking. Good qualities such as honesty, truthfulness, strong will power, attachment to God, and charitable nature are present in the personality of a person with good thinking. On the other hand, in a person with bad thoughts, the qualities of egoistic, greedy, cruel, and destructive tendencies, etc. are formed. Similarly, here karma means physical power, i.e., body texture and body's ability to do work. The four divisions are as follows: 1. Intelligent class (Brahmins), 2. Administrative class (Kshatriyas), 3. Merchant class (Vaishya), and 4. Service class (Shudras). If a Brahmin is given the job of a Kshatriya or Vaishya, he will fail. Similarly, if any person is given the work of some other department, instead of his department, then the system will collapse. **Lord Krishna**

has considered the distribution of work to be Karma Pradhan, that is, on the basis of doing work and not on the basis of the Birth. The universe has come into existence (took birth) only through Karma, and for the universe to survive, it has to work continuously. That's why karma is the main source of power for existence.

In this verse, Lord Krishna explained the wisdom of "Put the Right Man on the Right Job" thousands of years ago, to maintain the order of the society. In the context of modern management, it is called "Delegation." It is one of the important concepts of management. Delegation is one of the most important skills that a manager should have. Overworked and tired managers are often those people who don't know what delegation is and how to do it. A person's ability to do things on their own in a day is limited. But through delegation, he can achieve much more. In modern times, no industry or institution can run smoothly and effectively without the delegation process.

Now the question arises as to which work should be delegated and which should not. The work in which the level of competence is 8/10 should be taken to 9/10 or 10/10, and the work in which the level of competence is 3/10 should be delegated. Delegation means giving such work to another person who has the proficiency to do it properly.

Akbar is called The Great in history because he created Navratnas. He ruled the country smoothly and effectively. This is a beautiful historical example of Delegation.

It is important to note that, in the process of delegation, the responsibility for the result of the work is on the delegator and not on the delegatee. Therefore, while delegating, the responsibility of the work should be handed over only to the qualified, right person.

"DELEGATOR IS RESPONSIBLE, NOT THE DELEGATEE."

Verse: 4.34

Verse: Tadviddhi Pranipaten Pariprashnen Sevaya |
Upadekshyanti Te Gyanam Gyaninastattvadarshinah || 34 ||

Meaning: You can know this by serving the wise who knows the truth and by humbly asking questions again and again with prudence. They will definitely satisfy your curiosity.

In this verse Krishna describes the importance of knowledge for all. The method of learning and the importance of teacher–pupil relationship have been highlighted. Lord Shri Krishna says that there are three conditions to receive knowledge from the teacher: Firstly, the disciple should surrender himself to the teacher with faith and devotion. Second is staying near him, obeying him, and serving him. Thirdly, until the subject is understood, the disciple should keep asking questions politely to the teacher. Just as the milk starts flowing in the udders of a cow after seeing the affection of the calf, similarly, seeing the spirit of dedication and service in a disciple, an ocean of knowledge rises in the heart of the teacher to educate the disciple.

In the context of modern management, Lord Krishna has explained about the "Principles of Learning" in this verse. For the development of society, success of institutions, and personal happiness, education is essential. Deep desire to learn is fulfilled by approaching the Teacher. This verse is a guide on how to move ahead in career for the employees working in modern industries. The method is to surrender to your leader and honestly follow the guidelines given by him. Do the work. If you don't understand something, ask questions politely and get clarifications. This way trust grows and progress continues.

There is great power in curiosity. Curiosity has led to great research and discoveries in the world. The listening to Bhagavatam-Katha started with questions. There is a mythological story about it:

The story of Maharaj Parikshit listening to Bhagavatam:

According to the Mahabharata, Maharaja Parikshit was the grandson of Arjun, the son of Abhimanyu and Uttara, and the father of Janamejaya. Parikshit was a great king. Because of a crime, Parikshit Maharaj was cursed because that he would die in seven days. Considering the sage's curse as unalterable, when death drew near, he made Janamejaya sit on the throne and left the kingdom and went near Haridwar. Upon reaching there, he asked what should be done by a person whose death is near. People didn't say anything. Rishi Shukdev had also come there. When Parikshit came to know about Shukdev Goswami, he went to him and asked the same question. Shukdev Rishi said: He should listen to Bhagavatam. Parikshit said: Gurudev! Will you recite Bhagavatam for me? Shukdevji accepted his request. Parikshit Maharaj sat there, and Shukdev swami started reciting the Bhagavatam Purana. Along with him, 50,000 sages were also sitting there. Everyone listened to the Bhagavatam Purana for seven days and seven nights.

Gururbrahma Guruvishnu, Gururdevo Maheshwara |
Gurur Sakshat Par Brahma, Tasmai Shree Guruve Namah ||

- Skand Puran

Guru kumhar shisu kumbh hai, gadi gadi katai khot,
Antar haath sahar de Bahar bohe chot |

- Sant Kabir

Verse: 4.39

Verse: Shraddhavanllabhate Gyanam Tatparah Sanyatendriyah |
Jnanam Labdhwaa paraam Shantimchirenadhigachchhati ||39||

Meaning: The person who has faith, who is eager to acquire knowledge, who has controlled his senses, and who has the right to know immediately attains spiritual peace.

Lord Krishna says that the darkness of ignorance should be dispelled with the light of knowledge. To gain knowledge, control over the senses and devotion to the teacher are necessary. Only when you listen carefully to the teacher, you gain knowledge, and great things happen.

Swami Prabhupadaji Maharaj, after receiving learnings from his teacher, propagated that knowledge, the knowledge of Bhagavad Gita, all over the world. He had to struggle a lot to do this pious work but got success in the end. The whole life of Prabhupadaji Maharaj is inspirational.

Swami Srila Prabhupadaji Maharaj:

Swami Srila Prabhupada was a patriot and a devotee of Lord Krishna. In 1922, when he met his spiritual teacher Bhakti

Siddhanta Saraswati Thakur, he gave only one instruction: You are educated, so propagate the knowledge of Bhagavad Gita to the whole world. Swami Prabhupada founded "International Society for Krishna Consciousness" (ISKCON) in America in 1966 and spread the teachings of Lord Krishna all over the world. By 1976, 5.5 crore books in 25 languages reached all over the world. He wrote 22,000 pages, translated 18,000 verses in just 12 years, and used to work for 22 hours and rest for 2 hours.

Steve Jobs has written in his autobiography how he used to walk 7 kilometers every Sunday to go to ISKCON for lunch.

In this verse, in the context of modern management, Lord Krishna discusses the importance of 'knowledge' for a successful leader. With the power of knowledge, a man has complete control over his life. It is the source of power that differentiates man from other living beings in the universe. A wise person knows what is right and what is wrong. While writing on different styles of leadership, all management authors have recognized that "Knowledge" is a key component of the universal internal structure of the qualities of all great leaders of the world. "Keep on learning" is a lifelong endeavor for a leader. It is true that in reality a group of people is often dominated by the person who has the ability to clearly see the future.

"KNOWLEDGE IS POWER."

Vidvatvanch nripatvanch naiv tulyam kadachan |
Swadese Pujyate Raja Vidwaan sarwatra pujyate ||

(The king is worshiped only in his country, but the scholar is worshiped everywhere)

Verse: 4.40

Verse: Agyaschashrddhanasch Sanshayaatma Vinasyati |
Naym lokosti na paro na suksha samsyaatmanah ||40||

Meaning: One who is ignorant, who does not have faith, and who is suspicious is destroyed. For a slanderer, there is happiness neither in this world nor in the hereafter.

Lord Krishna says that a person who has no knowledge, no trace of faith, and is always in the circle of doubts, his destruction is certain.

In the context of modern management, Lord Krishna is emphasizing that trust and loyalty toward the organization is necessary. Employees who are not loyal to the organization and do not believe in their leader are fired from the job, and then they do not get a place in any other organization either. If there is any person in your organization (team) who does not have knowledge about the product, who thinks less about the organization and more about his own benefits, and is always surrounded by doubts about his gains in the organization, such a person is of no use. The destruction of such a person is certain.

CHAPTER-5

KARMA SANYAS YOGA (DEDICATING ALL ACTIONS TO GOD)

Preface:

In this chapter, Karma means Karma Yoga, and Sanyasa means Sankhya Yoga. Jnana Yoga, Sankhya Yoga, and Sanyasa are all synonymous. In this chapter, Lord Krishna has given a comparative sermon (discussion) on the facts of Karma Yoga and Jnana Yoga. Herein, there is a special description of the qualities of saints and their methodology.

Summary:

Arjun says: O Krishna! On the one hand, you praise giving up of work, i.e., renunciation (Sankhya Yoga), and on the other hand, you are preaching to do selfless work (Karma Yoga), i.e., to fight. O God! Tell me for sure which of the two is better for me.

Lord Shri Krishna says: Hey Partha! Jnana Yoga and Karma Yoga are two different paths, but their goal is the same, and by both the paths, the seeker attains the Divine. That's why both the yogas are perfect. But the practice of Sankhya Yoga based on knowledge is difficult. Compared to this, the practice of Karma Yoga is easy. Therefore, it is better to perform selfless actions (Karma Yoga) than to give up actions (Jnana Yoga).

A saint is not bound by any kind of relationship; he neither hates nor loves anyone. He does not have any desire. He remains composed in happiness and sorrow, winter and summer, success and failures, etc. Whether he works or not, he easily remains free from bondage (sin-virtue). Ignorant people consider Jnana Yoga and Karma Yoga to be different, but the wise do not. The goal of both the paths is the same—the realization of truth, i.e., the God, and both are considered the same.

O Arjun! Knowledge is not attained without hard work, and it is difficult to walk on the path of renunciation without knowledge. Whereas by the path of selfless Karma Yoga, by performing actions faithfully according to religion (morals), one can easily attain the Supreme Soul.

That's why O Arjun! **Because of the complexities and difficulties of the Sankhya Yoga (Saint Path), I have called Karma Yoga better.**

Lord Krishna further says the following about Karma Yoga: If a man works without any attachment, his soul remains pure. One who has controlled his senses, who considers all living beings as equal to himself, such a person never gets bound by the bondage of karma even while doing work. It means that he does not suffer any sin or virtue as a result of his actions. He feels detached even while speaking, walking, seeing, touching, etc. It is believed that his senses are self-controlled and perform all activities automatically according to their respective dharma (morals). He has no attachment to the fruits produced by the activities of the senses. In this way, the person who performs actions by renouncing attachment and dedicating the fruits of actions to God is not touched by sins, just as a lotus leaf remains untouched by water despite being in the pond.

O Arjun! The person who has practiced relinquishing attachment, when he performs any action, his body, mind, and intellect do not feel any attachment to the result of that action. He feels peace without ego. He has no attachment to the fruits produced by the activities of the senses. One who has renounced the fruits of actions lives happily in the city of nine gates (body).

Thereafter, Lord Krishna explains the essence of his teachings to Arjun: O Partha! Although God is present everywhere, He Himself does not act. God neither creates the doership of man, nor the action, nor the combination of the results of action. Every living entity, being subject to the laws of nature, does all this by itself under the influence of the prescribed modes of material nature. That's why the omnipresent God neither accepts anyone's sin nor anyone's virtue. Man himself is responsible for his sins and virtues. Humans whose intellect is clouded by the darkness of ignorance (pride, desires, greed, etc.) become unscrupulous. On the contrary, those who have overcome ignorance with their intellect in the light of knowledge see the divine in their soul and attain supreme happiness.

O Arjun! I am omnipresent, because I am present in the womb of this world. The wise with their knowledge see me everywhere and in every living being. I am in a learned Brahmin; I am in a Chandal (bad man); I am in a cow; I am in a dog; I am in an elephant; I am in an ant, and so on, i.e., I'm present everywhere.

Equanimity (Seeing God in Every Living Being)

Describing the characteristics of the wise, Lord Krishna says: O Arjun! As a man thinks, so he becomes. In every situation, for a man of equanimity, no one is alien to him, but he is in unity with all living beings and considers the whole world as his own. In this way, he becomes close to the Supreme Soul, because the Supreme Soul is omnipresent. He does not get pleased at those who love him and does not get angry at those who abuse him. His mind remains under his control, takes him inside the soul, makes him see the divine, and makes him feel the ecstasy.

O Arjun! Pleasure derived from the senses by chasing objects gives rise only to sorrow. The unattached man easily attains all happiness and peace by keeping the senses under control and seeing the divine in the soul within him.

Having said this much about Karma Yoga and Jnana Yoga, Shri Krishna has described the practices of Dhyana Yoga (Pranayama) performed by the ascetics for the attainment of the Supreme Soul. Lord says: O Arjun! Many people worship God with activities based on Pranayama to reach spiritual heights. In this sadhna (ritual), by diverting the attention from external objects, by fixating the vision between the eyebrows, and by equating the in and out breaths in the nostrils, people give offerings of the *prana vayu* in the *apana vayu*, and sometimes the apana vayu in the prana vayu. While doing this, the Yogi controls the senses, the mind, and the intellect; thereafter, there is a vision of God.

With the practice of Pranayama, man gets away from desires, lust, anger, greed, etc. When he peeps into his soul peacefully, he finds me the Maheshwar. He understands that I am the Lord of all, the friend of all, and the consumer of all sacrifices and penances.

MANAGEMENT CONCEPTS:

Verse: 5.18

Verse: Vidyavinayasampanne Brahmane Gavi Hastini |
Shuni Chaiv Shwapake Cha Panditah Samdarshinah || 18 ||

Meaning: A wise man sees the Brahmin, cow, elephant, dog, Chandal (the man who eats dog), and every living being equally. It means that everyone is treated equally (Equality towards Brahmin and Chandal means that when a Brahmin is bitten by a snake and the way a wise man tries to remove the poison by sucking the wound of a Brahmin, the same reaction will be applied when a Chandal is bitten by a snake.)

Lord Krishna says that a wise man does not make any distinction between different creatures, such as humans, elephants, birds, aquatic animals, ants, etc. Even among human beings, be it a Brahmin or a Chandal, rich or poor, irrespective of color or height, he considers all as equal. Physical differences are meaningless to him. He knows that the Supreme Soul, i.e., the Almighty, is present in all creatures without any discrimination. That's why a wise man looks at everyone equally, no matter who they are and whatever level they are at.

In the context of modern management, Lord Krishna has explained about "Team Management and Group Dynamics" in this verse. He says that like the wise man in this verse, a team leader should treat all the members of the organization equally. Good team management depends upon the team leader, how beautifully he executes work, ruling the group and creating harmony amongst themselves. The success of an organization depends on how good and effective the team management is. When the team leader treats all the members of the group equally without any discrimination, the members feel important, trust each other, and take responsibility for collective decisions. Their work efficiency increases, and the organization starts getting good results.

To understand team management, let us look at a mythological story of Ramayan.

Story of Ramayana: Ram Setu and the Squirrel

When Lord Shri Ram came to know that Ravana has imprisoned Sita in Lanka, he decided to attack Lanka. Lanka was an island surrounded by sea from all sides. To reach there, a bridge had to be built over the sea. The monkeys said, O Lord! We will help. The monkey army gets engaged in the work of building the bridge. To build a bridge, they picked up big stones and started throwing them in the sea and started chanting Jai Shri Ram. The rocks began to float instead of sinking in the sea. Seeing this, the monkey army became happy and started throwing rocks with full zeal and zest. Lord Rama was very happy to see the enthusiasm, dedication, and passion of his army to build the bridge.

At the same time, a small squirrel came there. She picks up a pebble in her mouth and leaves it on the bridge. She started doing this again and again. Seeing her doing this repeatedly, some monkeys got annoyed. They said, "O squirrel! You are so small, stay away from the sea. Don't let it happen that you get buried under these stones." Hearing all this, the squirrel becomes sad. Lord Rama was also watching all this from a distance. The squirrel went to Lord Rama crying and complained about the monkeys. Lord Rama called the monkey army. He showed that

Ram Setu Construction and Squirrel

the pebbles thrown by the squirrel were helping bind the big rocks. Lord Rama said, "If the squirrel had not thrown these pebbles, all the rocks thrown by you would have been scattered here and there. It is the pebbles thrown by the squirrel that hold them together. Squirrel's contribution to building the bridge is as invaluable as that of the members of the monkey army."

Having said all this, Lord Ram lovingly picked up the squirrel in his hand and stroked his fingers gently over her back. Since then, it is believed that the white stripes present on the body of the squirrels are nothing but the marks of Lord Rama's fingers.

Together, the monkeys constructed a 30-km-long and 3-km-wide bridge in just five days.

This is a great example of team management.

CHAPTER-6

DHAYAN YOGA (CONTACT WITH THE DIVINE)

Preface:

In this chapter, Lord Krishna has described an easy yogic practice called Pranayama, to meditate on the God. It is a simple and easy process of meditating on God by concentrating the mind. It is possible that it may be difficult for the general public to do meditation and yoga; at such a time, God has considered it best to do selfless work.

Summary:

Lord Krishna says: O Arjun! The person who, without desiring the fruits of action, continues to do the work that he should do is called a *sanyasi* (saint) and is also called a yogi. The one who gives up work and sits idle and does nothing is called lazy. No one can survive without working. It is most important to stop the horses of the mind, which keep chasing the lust of the senses. To give up the desires that focus day and night on worldly pleasures. Such a person is said to have attained the same level as a true Yogi achieves after a long process of continuous pranayama. That's why only **the one who does selfless work is a true Yogi.**

Man does good or bad by himself. He himself becomes his enemy and becomes his friend. The one who has conquered the mind is his own friend; the one who has not conquered the mind is his own enemy. The identity of the one who conquers the mind is that he remains the same in every situation of life, i.e., cold and heat, happiness and sorrow, profit and loss, honor and dishonor, and never gets distracted. A yogi is one who has wisdom, control over the senses, and for whom gold, soil, or stone are all equal. He has the same feelings toward enemy and friend, good man and bad man, etc.

Lord Krishna says: O Arjun! The purpose of meditation is to contact the Divine. A part of the Divine, that is the soul, rules within the human being. Contact with this soul is the first step to meet the Lord. That's why O Arjun! One who wants to meet me must first of all look within himself, and this can be possible only when one's own body is under his control. If the body is not under control, then the purpose of meditation will not be achieved. Listen, Arjun! Man should, sitting in solitude, concentrate his mind on the Lord. Because in solitude man can easily peep within himself. The place where meditation is performed should also be neat and clean.

O Arjun! While meditating on me, one should sit motionless, keeping his back, head, and neck even and straight. And fix the vision on the front part of your nose in such a way that all other directions disappear. By doing this, his senses will be cut off from the environment around him. Then, man will easily be able to peep into his own conscience.

Hey, Arjun! Such a man, who does not have balance in his life, will not be able to meditate on me. To be successful in meditation, one must be an observer of equanimity. My devotee should not eat so much that he should feel as if he is living only to eat. Nor eat so little that the bone structure is weakened. Don't sleep so much that you consider day as night; don't sleep so little that you don't consider night as night. If you get happiness, don't start dancing, and if you get sorrow, don't cry and become grief-stricken. A person who does not get extinguished by the gusts of the wind of sorrow and happiness is like the flame of a lamp kept in a vacuum, which remains straight and unshakable even in strong wind. At such a time, his mind is under his control, and then this mind takes the man into the soul and makes him have the vision of God.

Arjun says: O Madhusudan! It is very easy to say that you must control the mind, become the master of the mind, but this is the most difficult task. O Keshav! The mind is as fickle as the wind. Just as it is impossible to control the blowing wind, it is very difficult to control the fickle mind.

Lord Krishna explains: O Arjun! What you say is true that the mind is too fickle. It is definitely difficult to control the mind but not impossible. It can be controlled by Abhyasa (practice) and Vairagya (mortification or dispassion). Abhyasa means to continuously do what is proper (as per morals), and Vairagya means not to do what is improper (cravings for lust). The person who is constantly persistent in this kind of performance definitely gets success.

Arjun again asked: O Keshav! Suppose a man has faith in his

mind, but due to slow effort, he does not succeed. What is the fate of such a person? Doesn't he get destroyed like scattered clouds?

Lord Krishna clears the doubt and says: O Arjun! Such a person, after death, after settling in heaven according to his deeds, returns to earth and takes birth in a noble family. In his mind, the developed virtues of previous births are present. From here, starting the journey of his new life, he strives for the supreme goal of attaining the Lord. By making efforts like this, some quickly and some after many births, according to the strength of their faith and effort, attain the Lord.

In the end, Lord Krishna says: O Arjun! A Karma yogi who works selflessly is greater than the ascetics, sages, and the scholars of the scriptures. He is greater than the people who perform rituals. That's why, O Arjun! You become a Karma yogi and fight.

MANAGEMENT CONCEPTS:

Verse: 6.5 and 6.6
Verse: Uddaredatmanaatmanam Naatmanamvasadayet |
Atmaiva Hyatmano Bandhuratmaiva Ripuratmanah || 5 ||

Meaning: Man should improve himself with the help of his mind and should not let himself fall down. This mind is man's friend as well as enemy.

Verse: Bandhuratmātmanastasyayenaatmaivatmanajitah |
Anatmanastu Shatrutve Varteatmaiva Shatruvat || 6 ||

Meaning: For one who has conquered the mind, the mind is the best friend, but for the one who has not been able to do so, the mind will remain the worst enemy.

Lord Krishna says that each person is himself responsible for the ups and downs in his life. Whatever happens to him, it cannot be blamed on anyone else. Man should always try to raise his level by keeping the mind under control, through good thinking and good deeds. And in any situation, do not let the senses dominate the mind. It is necessary to win the mind. A conquered mind is like the best friend who leads a man toward the pinnacle of success. Defeated mind is like an enemy which keeps on pushing man toward the pit of sin.

You must have heard many people saying, "Friend, I am the king of the mind. I do what my mind tells me." This is a foolish statement. That person is not the king of the mind but slave of the mind. He did what the mind told him, so how is he the king of the mind. In fact, he became a slave. For example: Exams are going on. The mind says that there is a good movie, let's go and enjoy. In such a situation, if one goes to watch a movie, he has become a slave to the mind, because at that time the right thing to do is to prepare for the exams and get success.

In the context of modern management, in this verse, Lord Krishna has told about a psychological technique to mold the mind, that is, "need to mold the mind in such a way that it leads us on the right path." Today's modern psychology believes that you can control your mind by giving instructions. These instructions, in terms of psychology, are called auto-suggestions. Auto-suggestions affect both the conscious and the sub-conscious mind. The conscious mind has the ability to think. It can accept or reject. But the subconscious mind only accepts. Auto-suggestion is a way of molding your subconscious mind into the mold you want. Auto-suggestion is a process of repetition. If you repeat a statement over and over again, it gets embedded in your subconscious mind, and your attitude and behavior start changing accordingly.

The brain follows the computer principle, i.e., GIGO (Garbage in, Garbage out), meaning that whatever goes in the mind is what comes out.

Negativity inside; Negativity out
Positivity Inside; Positivity out
Good inside; Good out

Auto-suggestions should be positive statements that are phrased in a positive way.

To understand this, let us take the example of learning to ride a bicycle. We all remember how we learned to ride a bicycle. First, the child repeatedly practices riding the bicycle at the level of the conscious mind. With repeated practice, the art of learning starts settling in the subconscious mind of the child. Gradually, the child learns to ride a bicycle with full understanding so well that he no longer has to think consciously. While riding a bicycle, he can even talk to people and wave at others. This means that the ability to ride a bicycle is already ingrained in his subconscious mind. There is no need to pay attention and think at this level because it is embedded automatically into his behavior.

Lord Krishna is suggesting bringing all good habits to the level of the subconscious mind by auto-suggestions.

Let's take a look at the events happening around us.

Most of the suicides occur in technologically advanced and developed countries like Germany, South Korea, Japan, the U.S.A., etc. America is a prosperous and powerful country in every way. They have overcome all kinds of difficulties. Despite all this, today, every second American, i.e., 50% of the population, visits a psychiatrist at least once a year. A psychiatrist sees so many patients in a day that by the evening he himself feels the need of a psychiatrist. In developed countries, the most confusing day is called "Father's Day." Half the people are confused as to whom I should go and say "Happy Father's Day," and the other half are worried that someone might come and say "Happy Father's Day" to them.

In India, Bangalore Mini Silicon Valley, where most of the intellectual class works, is slowly becoming a suicide city. Do you know why? Because they are moving fast but in the wrong direction.

The reason for all these problems is **"Lack of Mind Control."** People are becoming directionless.

Let us see what is happening in the schools. We all know that children are playful and mischievous by nature. Earlier they used to play with chalk, used to distract the attention of teachers, used to eat tiffin in ongoing class, used to hide someone's belongings, used to quarrel with each other and later used to play together, etc. Today, the three most serious problems in schools are profanity, i.e., abusive language, drug addiction, and teen pregnancy. Students shooting and killing teachers and classmates has become a major crisis. Everyone is worried. Why?

All this is happening because of **"Lack of Mind Control."**

Don't Take Dictation of the Mind,
Give Dictation to the Mind.

- Dr. Vivek Bindra

Until you realize how easy it is for your mind to be manipulated,
You remain a puppet of someone else's game.

- Evita Ochet

Verse: 6.7

Verse: Jitatmanah Prashantasya Parmatma Samahitah |
Shitosnsukaduhkheshu Tatha Manapamanayoh || 7 ||

Meaning: One who has conquered his mind and attained peace has attained God, because for such a man, happiness and sorrow, cold and heat, and honor and disgrace are all equal.

Lord Krishna says that when a man's mind is engulfed by illusory illusions, it gets entangled in material activities. But as soon as the mind comes under control, man is considered to have reached the goal. By controlling the mind, a man starts doing good deeds. He doesn't get distracted by the obstacles of happiness and sorrow, cold and heat, honor and insult, etc. coming in the way and keeps moving toward the goal. It is said that the mind of such a person is under his control.

Mind control is necessary to move forward in life. If you learn to control your mind, you can do great things in life. Great leaders throughout history, like Swami Vivekananda, Mahatma Gandhi, Guru Nanak, Winston Churchill, Abraham Lincoln, etc., had conquered their mind and left the world doing great things.

Those who cannot control the mind have a weak belief

system. Usually, such people are convinced of their weaknesses, get used to living with them, and remain in trouble for the whole life. On the contrary, people who have control over their mind do more work beyond their capacity and remain happy throughout their life.

To understand this issue let us look at these stories.

1. Story of the Elephant and the Rope:

Think of a huge elephant that is made accustomed to being tied to one place by a thin rope and a peg, while he is so strong that he can easily uproot the peg and roam wherever he wants. This is because, in childhood, the elephant is tied to a strong chain and to a strong tree. Both the chain and the tree are much stronger than the baby elephant. The child is not used to being chained, so he constantly tries unsuccessfully to pull and break the chain. There comes a day when the child understands that there is no use in trying to pull and break. He stops and starts to stand still. Now he is mentally used to it. And when the same child becomes a huge elephant, it is tied with a weak rope and stake. If that elephant wants, it can be freed only by giving a blow, but now it does not go anywhere because it has been mentally accustomed to it since childhood. His master has instilled in him a weak belief system.

2. Story of a Bumblebee:

We can learn a lot if we carefully observe the nature around us. God has done amazing feats in the creation of nature. Take the example of a bumblebee. Scientists say that the body of a bumblebee is too heavy, and the spread of its wings is too small for it to be able to fly. According to the theory of flying (Aerodynamics), the bumblebee, in any way, cannot fly. But the bumblebee doesn't know this and keeps on flying.

When we do not know our limits and limitations, we go out and surprise ourselves by doing great things. Looking back, we often wonder if we had any limitations to begin with. The only limitations a person has are those that are self-imposed. Like the elephant created its own boundaries and stands silently. On the other hand, the bumblebee has no knowledge of its limit, so it keeps flying freely.

Verse: 6.17

Verse: Yuktaharviharasya Yuktachestasya Karmasu |
Yuktswapnavabodhasya yogo bhavati dukhaha || 17 ||

Meaning: The person who eats and drinks in a limited quantity (neither more nor less), who has regulated his habits, whose sleep and wakefulness are regular, such a discipline when comes in him, destroys sorrows.

Lord Krishna says: The body is the medium for doing all the work of a man, whether it is to get education, to practice yoga, to do charity in the society, or to worship God. Everywhere, the body is present and works. That's why it becomes necessary that a man should take special care of his body and remain healthy. After keeping the body healthy, the next main step is to acquire continuous knowledge, i.e., to keep up the process of continuous learning.

Lord Krishna also shared the way to keep the body healthy. Eating, drinking, sleeping, staying awake, protecting, roaming around, entertainment, etc. are physical needs and should be fulfilled in a measured manner. That is, man should neither eat too much nor too little; sleep neither too much nor too little, etc. By this process, the body remains healthy, and it becomes easy to acquire knowledge. Yoga practice becomes easy. It becomes easy to control the mind and devote to God. A body ridden by diseases is of no use.

In the context of modern management, Lord Krishna explained the wisdom and necessity of "Mental development by acquiring knowledge while keeping the body healthy." From the perspective of management, it is called "Sharpen Your Axe," which is a very important Management Principle. Stephen R. Covey, in his book "The 7 Habits of Highly Effective People," elaborates on this principle in the seventh point. Sharpen your axe means enhancing personal utility while renewing oneself by creating a balanced strategy in the areas of the physical, social, mental, and spiritual. Some examples of these activities are as follows:

Physical: Eating healthy, Exercising, Resting

Social: Having social and meaningful relationships with others

Mental: Reading, Writing, Teaching, Learning

Spiritual: Spending time in nature, Meditation, Music, Art, Prayer, or Service

Sharpening your axe refreshes you, increases your ability to deliver results and take on the challenges around you. Without this renewal the body becomes weak, the mind mechanical, the emotions raw, the soul insensitive, and the individual selfish.

Let us look at the story of a woodcutter.

Story of a Woodcutter:

A woodcutter named Peter was working for a company for many years. He never got promoted. That company also hired a new woodcutter, Smith. Smith got a promotion within a year. Peter sadly went to his master and asked the reason. The owner said that you cut as many trees as you used to cut before. Our company looks at results. If you cut more trees, your salary will also be raised. Peter went and worked hard, but there was no result. He couldn't cut more trees. Once again he went to the owner and told his problem. The owner advised: You go and meet Smith. Peter went to Smith and told him the problem. He asked Smith, "How do you cut more trees?" Smith said, "After cutting down every tree, I stop for five minutes and sharpen the axe. When was the last time you sharpened your axe?" Peter got the answer. He too started sharpening his axe and soon got promoted.

The learning process is very important in life. Let us look to this story of Ramayana when Lord Ram asked Lakshmana to go to Ravana to acquire some learnings.

Ravana in his Last Moments of Life Gave Lessons to Lakshman:

At the time when Ravana was lying on earth in the state of near death, Rama said to Lakshman, "Ravana, a great scholar of political science, is leaving this world. You go and take some lessons from this great scholar." As per the order of Lord Rama, Lakshman went and stood near Ravana's head. Ravana did not say anything. Lakshman came back to Ram. Seeing this, Rama said, "Lakshman, learning is always received by sitting near the feet of the Guru." Lakshman went again and sat down at Ravana's feet. Ravana, a great sapient and scholar, told Lakshman these three invaluable lessons of life.

1. **Auspicious work should be done as soon as possible.**

2. **Enemy and disease should never be considered small.**

3. **The secret related to your life should be kept secret. It should not be told to any person, even if he is the dearest. Because relationships keep changing.** (Only Vibheeshan knew that there is nectar in Ravana's navel. This later became the cause of Ravana's death.)

**"Give me Six Hours to Chop Down a Tree,
And I Will Spend First Four Sharpening The Axe."**
- Abraham Lincoln

Verse: 6.19

Verse: Yatha Deepo Nivatastho Nengate Sopama Smrita |
Yogino Yatchittasya Yunjto Yogamatmanah || 19 ||

Meaning: Just as the flame of a lamp remains steady in a vacuum, similarly, when the mind of a Karma yogi is under his control, his mind is always steady in the meditation of God.

Lord Shri Krishna says: Man should discipline his mind with strong will power, so that no cravings for material desires or any other obstacles can distract him from the path of his goal. People with strong will power do great things in life.

In the context of modern management, Lord Krishna has given the lesson of "Will Power to Persist," a very important and high moral conduct necessary for successful leadership. This important quality has always been there in all the great leaders throughout history. Hundreds of difficulties arise in the implementation of any plan or project, and the people implementing the plan may also face failures. A good leader has a strong will power to stick to his goal despite all odds. This way, you definitely succeed.

Lord Krishna has also explained the way how to strengthen will power. The way is that a man should not run after physical and worldly pleasures; while keeping the mind under control, he should gradually strengthen his will power. Another successful way to keep the will power strong is fasting. It has been told in almost all the religions. Mahatma Gandhi was a great advocate of fasting. Following the path of truth and non-violence, he often fasted to keep his resolve, to free India; strong and without wavering, he finally achieved the freedom for India.

To understand this, let us look at the story of Swami Srila Prabhupada Ji Maharaj. He propagated the knowledge of the Bhagavad Gita, all over the world, despite all the obstacles.

Swami Srila Prabhupada Ji Maharaj's story:

Swami Prabhupada (1 September 1896–14 November 1977) was born in 1896 in Calcutta. He was named Abhyacharan Dey. His father brought him up as a Krishna devotee. Swami Prabhupada was a true patriot, and in 1922 supported Gandhiji in the Non-Cooperation Movement. Prabhupadaji was a disciple of Bhakti Siddhanta Thakur Saraswatiji. One day, Thakur Saraswatiji instructed Swami Prabhupada: You are brilliant; preach Lord Krishna's Bhagavad Gita through English language all over the world.

To follow his Guru's command, in 1965, at the age of 70, without money or any help, he left for America. After a 32-day sea voyage, he had only seven dollars left when he reached America. He started his mission from America's largest city New York (Tomkins Square Park). In those days a war was going on between America and Vietnam. In the wake of the Vietnam War, there was great despair among the youths of America. The hippie culture had taken a toll on society, especially in the youth segment. Hippies were those people who had rejected the mainstream life of America and lived in their own way. They had left their homes and swarmed the roads. Lived on the roads and streets, roamed naked, slept there, taking charas, ganja, and other drugs and were always intoxicated. They had no one to call their own. Above, the open sky, and below, the land, had become their world.

Swami Prabhupada thought that these are the most difficult people, lost in life. If with the knowledge of Bhagavad Gita, I convert them and help them get rid of their bad habits, make their life simple, then they will not only be benefited but also the whole world will acknowledge the Bhagavad Gita's superiority. After taking this decision, he started living with them. Hippies used to blow cigarette smoke on him, used to steal his food, his books, his typewriter, harassed him a lot, and made his life worse. Despite all the insults, Swamiji used to cook food for them morning and evening, give medicines, and tell stories. Braving all kinds of difficulties, Swami Prabhupada remained steadfast in his purpose, without wavering. Seeing his selfless spirit of service and boundless stamina, the hearts of the hippies finally melted. They gave up all bad habits of smoking cigarettes, taking drugs, and eating meat and became disciples of Swamiji. Gradually, there was a change in them, and everyone started reciting Bhagavad Gita. The American Government was very happy with this great work of Swamiji and praised him a lot.

In 1966, Swamiji founded the International Society for Krishna Consciousness (ISKCON). He made incense sticks and started selling them. He built a small temple with the money he earned. He started teaching Bhagavad Gita, and started writing and selling books.

The work that Swamiji has done in the world, no one else could have done. By 1977, in just 12 years, over 65 million books had been delivered worldwide in 32 languages. He toured the world 14 times and preached Bhagavad Gita everywhere. As earlier mentioned, he used to work for 22 hours, rest for 2 hours. Swamiji founded the world's largest publishing house on spiritual books — Bhakti Vedanta Book Trust.

Swami Prabhupada single-handedly propagated the knowledge of Bhagavad Gita all over the world and inspired people to a new life. He removed the darkness of ignorance from people's lives and enlightened them with knowledge.

Verse: 6.26

Verse: Yato yato nischlati manashchanchalamsthiram |

Tatastato Niyammaytadatmanyave Vasham Naye || 26 ||

Meaning: Wherever the mind wanders due to its fickleness and unsteadiness, a man should pull it from there and bring it under his control.

Lord Krishna says: The mind is fickle and unstable by nature. That's why no matter whatever effort a man has to make, he should keep the mind under control. Focusing on where a man wants to go in life, that is, what his goal is, he should put all his energy in achieving that goal. The mind will try a lot to divert you from the path; it will tempt you in various ways, but without being misled by the mind, you have to move ahead with determination on the path of your goal. From the beginning of the work till the destination, all the focus should be on the goal. This is possible only when the mind remains under your control.

Lord Krishna has informed about the way to "Move ahead keeping the goal in mind." In the context of modern management, this is called "Begin with the End in Mind." Stephen R. Covey, in his book "The 7 Habits of Highly Effective People," explains this principle in detail in the second point. This is a very important quality of a visionary leader.

Starting with the end in mind means starting with a clear destination in mind. It means knowing where you are going, so that you can better understand where you are now, so the steps you take are always in the right direction. If you don't make this conscious effort to visualize who you are and what you want in life, then other people and circumstances decide and shape your life. Then, slowly, you cease to exist.

If your ladder isn't leaning against the right wall, every step you take is going to take you to the wrong place, and fast.

People usually say that time flies. If time is an aeroplane, we are the pilots. If we don't know our goals, someone else is the pilot and we are the passengers.

To understand this point, let us look at this story.

Watch and Compass:

Once you're flying in a plane, the captain's voice over the public address system says, "We've got good news and bad news. The good news is that the winds are favorable; we'll be there an hour early. And the bad news is that the navigation system is broken, and we don't know where the plane is going." He says: Take a parachute and jump. You jump and land in the forest. The only way out of the jungle is to run south. How do you know which direction is the south? You have two options to choose from — a watch or a compass. Of course, you will choose compass.

"Your Direction Is More Important Than Your Speed."
- Richard L. Evans

Verse: 6.34 and 6.35

Verse: Chanchalanhi Manah Krishna Pramathi Balvaddridham |
Tasyaham Nigraham Manye Vayoriv Sudushkaram ||34||

Meaning: Arjun says: O Krishna! Since the mind is fickle, disorderly, obstinate, and extremely strong, I find it more difficult to subdue it than to subdue the wind.

Verse: Asanshayam Mahabaho Mano Durnigraham Chalam |
Abhyasen Tu Kaunteya Vairagyena Cha Ghriyate ||35||

Meaning: Lord Krishna said: O Mahabaho son of Kunti! Undoubtedly, it is very difficult to control the fickle mind, but it is possible to control it by suitable Abhyas (practice) and Vairagya (dispassion).

At many instances in the Bhagavad Gita, Lord Krishna has talked about raising the standard of life by controlling the mind. The mind, being surrounded by the senses, always tries to divert a man toward material pleasures. It is not easy to discipline the mind. Even a brave warrior like Arjun is worried about the same thing. He tells Lord Krishna that he can control all the great things of the world, even the wind, but the mind is so fickle and stubborn that it is very difficult to control. "O Vasudev! You suggest a way." Krishna said: O Arjun! Controlling the mind is difficult but not impossible. The fickle mind can be tamed by constant Abhyas and Vairagya. Abhyasa means to do what is right to achieve the goal, and Vairagya (renunciation) means to not do what is wrong to achieve the goal.

In the context of modern management, Lord Krishna has explained about "Need and Importance of Discipline" in life. In today's management science, among the qualities of leadership, discipline is considered the most important and essential quality. Lord Krishna has also shared the method of how to bring discipline into practice. The method is: do those things which help in achieving the goal and don't do those things which create obstacles.

Henri Fayol was a French mining engineer and management theorist. He is also known as "The Father of Modern Management Theory." He discussed 14 principles of management in his 1916 book "General and Industrial Management." Discipline has been described as one of those principles. Management expert and great motivational speaker, Shiv Khera, says: Discipline is a track to move on. If you remove the train from the track, where does it go? Nowhere. While sitting in the plane, everyone wants that the plane should be run by such a pilot who is disciplined and works according to the control tower. You must have seen that many people do not reach the goal in life; they face defeat and crisis again and again, while some people keep succeeding. The reason for this is discipline. Without discipline, no one could ever achieve significant success in any field of life.

To understand discipline, let us look at this story.

Story of the Kite Without String:

Once, a father and son went to a kite flying festival. Seeing the kites, the son asked the father for a kite and a roll of thread. He too wanted to fly a kite. The father bought a kite and a roll of thread for the son.

The son started flying the kite, and soon it was flying high in the sky. The father asked, "Who is flying your kite?" The son said, "The wind is flying the kite." Father asked, "And what is the thread doing?" The son said, "It seems that the thread is stopping the kite from flying high." Father said ok and then cut the thread. The kite went a little higher but then slowly started coming down and fell on the ruins of a building. The son was surprised. He said, "I thought that after cutting the thread, the kite could fly high freely. But it fell down."

The father explained: Son, the thread was not stopping the kite from going higher, rather it was helping the kite to stay at the same height when the wind slowed down. When the wind is strong, the kite reaches a new height by moving in the right direction with the help of the thread. Without the support of the thread, the kite slowly falls down. This thread is like discipline, with the help of which the kite can touch new heights.

Just like the thread, with the help of discipline, a man can also reach the heights of success like a kite. Discipline is necessary to do great things in life.

JNANA VIJNANA YOGA (NATURE OF GOD)

Preface:

In the previous chapters, on many occasions Lord Krishna has told Arjun that man should take refuge in God. But what is the form of God? Until and unless the face, color, size, or any form of identity of God is known, it is not easy to meditate on Him and concentrate the mind. To the common man it seems impossible. Two forms of God have been explained in this chapter. One form is called Jnana, which means amorphous (nirgun-nirakar), i.e., having no definite shape, form, or structure, or say, formless. The second form is called Vijnana, which means corporeal (sagun-sakar), i.e., tangible. Man can meditate by keeping any form of God in his mind according to his intellect. The worship of the Lord in the corporeal form, i.e., tangible form, is simple and perfect. In this chapter, the Lord begins to give the knowledge of devotional service.

Summary:

Lord Krishna says: O Partha! Now I will tell you that if a man practicing Karma Yoga comes under my shelter, then how he can recognize me completely. After this knowledge, there is nothing left to know. Out of thousands, only a few try to achieve it, and among those who try, only a few are successful.

Lord Krishna says: O Arjun! My form is made of two natures (Nature is called prakriti in Sanskrit, also meaning Maya Shakti/illusory power of God). First nature is called "jada," i.e., foundation or body. This is made up of eight-fold elements called earth, water, sky, fire, air, mind, intelligence, and ego. All these make up our body. The second nature is the living form, which is called "consciousness." Out of these two natures, i.e., the relationship of the "body" and the "consciousness," the whole world exists. Just understand that they are the building blocks of all that is in this world. All living beings are born from this.

I am the creator of the whole world and also the destroyer. Just as the beads of a rosary are strung on its thread, similarly, the whole world is held on my base (thread). For example, I am the juice in water; I am the Omkar of the Vedas; I am the sound of the sky; I am the prowess of men; I am the fragrance in the soil; I am the radiance of fire; I am the life of every living being; I am the penance of the ascetic; I am the wisdom of the wise; I am the strength of the strong. In short, understand that I am present everywhere in the whole world.

O Arjun! A human being is born with the three qualities (gunas) of sattva, rajas, and tamas within him since birth. The world has been created on the basis of these three qualities.

Falling under the delusion of this triple illusion of mine, people do not recognize me, the imperishable. It is difficult to conquer this illusion of mine, but those who take refuge in me can cross this illusion.

O Arjun! There are four types of my devotees. One is those who are in trouble; the other is the curious; the third are the ones who are desirous of wealth, and the fourth is the wise. Although all are very good, the wise are the best. The wise is the one who always wants to join me while performing selfless duty. He is very dear to me. After rounds of many births of practice, when he comes to know that there is nothing else in this whole universe except me, "The Vasudeva," he finally finds me. But O Arjun! Such a wise man or Mahatma is still rare.

Arjun asks, "O Madhusudan! Different people in the world worship different gods. So is it a sin?"

Lord Krishna explains: No, Partha! Worship is never a sin, and the creatures who worship different gods, all of them, in fact, worship me. Therefore, whatever deity a man worships with devotion, with the desire for fruits, I establish that man's faith in that deity. I am the one who gives the result of one's devotion. People of low intellect, who worship me for the sake of enjoyment, get perishable fruits which are destroyed shortly after enjoying. The devotee, who meditates on me with devotion, worships me, only he reaches to me.

Lord says: O Partha! I am unborn and eternal. Being surrounded by my Yoga Maya, i.e., illusion, I do not appear before everyone. The vision of ordinary people cannot see beyond the veil of Maya. But without being enslaved by selfishness and attachment, crossing the darkness of illusion, the man who looks into his inner self, i.e., his soul, with the desire to connect with me, he finds me.

AKSHAR BRAHMA YOGA (DESCRIPTION OF THE ELEMENTS OF GOD)

Preface:

Both the words 'Akshara' and 'Brahma' are the names of the corporeal (Saguna, i.e., tangible) and amorphous (Nirguna, i.e., formless) forms of the Lord. Om is also one of the names of God. In this chapter, there is a description of God's Sagun form, Nirgun form, and Omkar. After learning about the complex design of the universe, Arjun asks some deep questions to better understand the nature of God. In this chapter, the Lord has provided a simple and easy way to learn about Him.

Summary:

Arjun asks: O Purushottam! You mentioned names like Param Brahma, Adhyatma, Karma, Adhibhuta, Adhidaiva, and Adhiyagya, but I did not understand their meanings. You also said that people who have controlled their mind can recognize you at the time of death. Please explain all this to me.

Lord replied: O Arjun! That which never perishes, which is always and will always be, is called Param Brahma. In other words, Param Brahma is known as The God, The Almighty, Parmatma, etc. The soul which takes on the body, which is the master of that body, is called Adhyatma (spirituality). Karma is the name of the creative power by which all things, including living beings, come into existence. All substances that are born and end are called Adhibhuta (supernumerary). According to the arrangement of Param Brahma, Brahma creates the whole world. All the gods and goddesses, the entire world, are included in His structure. Brahmaji has been called Adhidev. The indwelling God, who is in this body, is called Adhiyagya. In other words, Adhiyagya means The God Himself. O Arjun! Man takes his next birth with the same feelings and thoughts as the kind of thoughts and feelings he has in the last moments of his current life. At such a time, man should think about me with his mind and intellect. Only then he will find me. For this situation, a man should prepare in advance. At the time of death, the mind should not wander, should be engrossed in the devotion to God who dispels darkness like the sun. I believe that, with continuous practice and effort, man definitely gets inclined toward God.

Arjun says: O Yogeshwar! You answered many of my questions. I want to ask one more question. It is said that at the time of death a man has to suffer a lot. Whether the death is due to a wound by a weapon, or it comes naturally. Is there no way to make death easier?

Lord said: O Arjun! Life is not meant to make death easy, but to attain salvation by getting out of the cycles of life and death. If at the time of death, a man follows the method which I am going to tell you, then he will get salvation immediately. At the time of death, detached from the activities of the senses, when a man meditates on God, by concentrating the mind on God, holding the breath (for oxygen), and then slowly releasing it by pronouncing the word 'Om,' he definitely finds God. No matter how big a sinner a person has been throughout his life, following this process he can definitely attain salvation, i.e., he will come to my supreme abode.

Lord says: O Arjun! Man keeps making thousands of plans in his hundred years of life. But time is eternal. One day of Brahma is equal to the duration of a thousand yugas. The tenure of Brahma is of hundred years. In Brahma's day and night, creations and destructions go on, and will go on. In this cycle of eternal time, the life of man is just a moment. So, why so much fuss about this little time? In this short life, only faith in God is appropriate. Running after momentary pleasures is not fair. Over and above the Brahma's creation of repeated cycles of life and death, there is a place where things do not perish. This is the abode of the imperishable God, which is called "Paramdham." The one who attains God is freed from the cycles of life and death. His sight is possible only through exclusive devotion. God is omnipresent, and by His power the whole world continues.

(Sun stays in Uttarayan, i.e., Northern Hemisphere, for six months in a year and Dakshinayan, i.e., Southern Hemisphere, for the remaining six months. The fortnight of the waxing moon is called Shukla Paksha, and the fortnight of waning moon is called Krishna Paksha.)

Lord further explained: Hey Arjun! During the day, Shukla Paksha, and six months of Uttarayan—this is the time when the man who departs from the world finds God. During the night, Krishna Paksha, and six months of Dakshinayan—this is the time when the man who departs from this world is trapped in the cycles of life and death. Light and darkness, these two paths of the world are considered eternal. The one who goes from the first one does not return, whereas the one who goes from the second one comes back. O Arjun! Understand this in this way—the path of light is the path of selfless service, and the path of darkness is the path of selfishness. After knowing these two paths, who will choose the path of darkness, trapped in delusion? Man should choose the path of light while doing selfless duty.

MANAGEMENT CONCEPTS:

Verse: 8.5 and 8.6

Verse: Antakale Cha Mamev Smaranmuktava Kalevaram |
Yah Prayati Sa Madbhavam Yaati Nastystra Sanshyah || 5 ||

Meaning: At the end of his life, he who renounces the body remembering me immediately attains my shelter. There is not even an iota of doubt in this.

Verse: Yam Yam Vaapi Smaranbhavam Tyajatyante Kalevaram |
Tam TamevaitiKunteya Sadatadbhavbhavitah || 6 ||

Meaning: O son of Kunti! Man takes the next birth according to the thoughts and feeling he remembers while leaving the body.

Lord Krishna says: Man's ability to think and remember is a very important quality. This is that mental power which first accepts the incidents happening around, or the things heard, and then stores it in some corner of the mind. When there is a need or a context or on seeing or hearing something similar to those incidents, it is recollected immediately. This is called the power to remember, i.e., Memory. As a person thinks, his behavior is determined accordingly. Incidents occur accordingly. His personality molds to his thinking. That's why man should keep improving his thinking and thoughts so that his nature and personality become good and flourish. Lord Krishna says: One takes the next birth according to one's thoughts at the time of death. The good deeds done in this birth go to the next birth, and then in the next birth, they are generated by making a place in some corner of his mind. The remembrance of a particular emotion at the time of death is not a momentary process. It takes a lifetime of practice. A person's life-long thoughts, being accumulated, influence his thinking process at the time of death.

From the perspective of modern management, Lord Krishna is teaching a psychological method of increasing the capacity of the brain through good thought-process. Today's psychology believes that by practicing auto-suggestions, your subconscious mind can be molded into the desired mold. By increasing the capacity of the brain, a man can do wonders. Dale Carnegie's 1936 book "How to Win Friends and Influence People" states that we only use 10% of our brain's potential. It is implicitly suggested that by using the remaining potential, one can increase one's intelligence. The level of intelligence of Albert Einstein and Swami Vivekananda was much above that of an average person. Swami Vivekananda used to remember

Gajendra-Moksha

a book after reading it only once. Management expert and world famous great motivational speaker, Dr. Vivek Bindra calls it "Leadership Remodeling." This is an important leadership quality. This quality has always been there in the personality of all the great leaders in history. To build good habits, successful people keep refining their thoughts. Apart from this, your thinking can also be changed by reading the nature and behavior of other successful people. This is an ongoing process.

Let us listen to the mythological story of Gajendra to understand this point.

Gajendra-Moksha Story:

In a dense forest there lived the mighty chieftain Gajendra, along with many elephants. One day, Gajendra was walking with the herd. Distressed by the scorching sun and thirst, he took his herd to the nearby lake to drink water. As soon as Gajendra started drinking water in the lake, a strong crocodile aggressively caught hold of his leg. Gajendra tried hard to free his leg, but all went in vain. Other elephants also tried a lot to free him, but they too could not do anything. Because it was his territory, i.e., the lake, the crocodile was more powerful. Sometimes Gajendra would pull the crocodile out, and sometimes the crocodile would drag him inside. Gajendra and the crocodile fought with all their might for a thousand years. Seeing this unique war, even the gods were surprised.

Being dragged for a long time in the water, Gajendra felt his body and mind weakened. The crocodile was aquatic, so it started pulling Gajendra with more enthusiasm and force.

In his previous birth, Gajendra was an ardent devotee of Lord

Vishnu. The spirit of worship, prayers, and devotion offered to Lord Vishnu in the previous birth was present in some corner of his mind even in this birth. That's why he remembered all those prayers. All the elephants had left him. Death was near. Then he cried out to Lord Vishnu: "O Lord, come and save me!" Hearing the devotee's compassionate call, God reached there running barefoot. He killed the crocodile with the Sudarshan chakra and saved Gajendra.

One gets the fruit as per the kind of feeling in his mind. Let us look at the following story.

False Saint:

A saint and a prostitute died on the same day. The saint is sent to hell and the prostitute to heaven. The saint protests against this. He was told that the prostitute was always thinking of the saintly man and was regretting her life. And the saint always kept thinking about the prostitute and the happiness with her. The saint asked about the effect of all the religious work performed in all the years. He was then shown that a large number of devotees were honorably cremating his body, whereas the body of the prostitute was being cremated as an orphan.

A man gets the next birth according to the mood he remembers while leaving the body. There is a beautiful story of Ajamil in Shrimad Bhagwat Purana in this context.

Ajamil, who was a part of hell, reached heaven by uttering the name of Narayan:

Ajamil was virtuous, intelligent, and a devotee of Vishnu.

Ajamil's Salvation

Obedient to his parents, the son duly studied the Vedas and scriptures till his adolescence. As soon as he entered youth, an incident happened to him that changed his whole life. One day, Ajamil was returning from the forest with the best fruits and flowers for worship as per his father's orders. On the way he saw a beautiful woman in a garden. He started looking at that woman. Trapped in the beauty of the woman, Ajamil even forgot his values. He threw the fruits and flowers kept for worship and fell in love with the woman and came home with her.

When the father got angry, he said that he had a Gandharva-Vivah (love marriage) with that woman. The father tried to make sense to him, but how could Ajamil, who was obsessed with the woman, understand? He threw his father out of the house. Having forgotten public shame, work, and rituals, Ajamil used to steal, loot, and rob to fulfil the wishes of the woman. He was addicted to alcohol and gambling. He started getting satisfaction only in bad deeds. Ajamil had nine children from that woman.

His wife became pregnant for the tenth time. Then one day a convoy of twenty-five saints was passing through the village of Ajamil. When it was evening, the saints camped in front of Ajamil's house. When Ajamil came in the night, he saw the saints in front of his house. He got furious and started abusing them. Hearing the noise, Ajamil's wife came there. She scolded the husband and pacified him. The next day the sages asked for dakshina from Ajamil. He again got furious and ran to hit the sages. His wife stopped him. The sages said that we do not want money. Ajamil said yes, then it is okay. The sages said that you should name your future son as "Narayan." This is our dakshina. When a son was born to Ajamil's wife, Ajamil named him Narayan and loved him.

Later on, when the end of Ajamil came near, the terrible Yamdoots (agents of the god of death) came to take him. Distraught with fear, Ajamil called out Narayan! Narayan! On hearing the name of the Lord, the messengers of Lord Vishnu immediately reached there. The messengers of Lord broke the rope with which the Yamdoots had tied Ajamil. On being asked by the Yamdoots, the messengers said that due to the effect of the name of Narayan, he is under refuge to Sri Hari. The Yamdoots had to leave Ajamil against the messengers of God. In this way, Ajamil attained salvation.

That's why it is said that salvation is attained only by taking the name of God.

CHAPTER-9

RAJ VIDYARAJ GUHYA YOGA (THE PATH OF DEVOTION)

Preface:

So far in the previous chapters, the Lord has placed Karma Yoga at the highest position. Now the glory of the Devotion remains to be discussed. The Karma yogi of the Gita is not a dry scholar, nor a celibate ascetic. In this chapter, God has preached to follow the path of devotion (or bhakti) and called it the king of all knowledge, i.e., the best wisdom. Bhakti means attachment to God or love for God. This is also the easiest way to practice detachment from physical or worldly pleasures. What is easily understood by the heart is called simple and what is not understood is called difficult. The path of devotion is the easiest way to attain God. This chapter explains that without devotion to the Lord, it is impossible to have detachment from the fruits, i.e., to become a true Karma yogi.

Summary:

Lord Krishna says: O Arjun! Now I will tell you the most secret knowledge. After understanding this, all the evil in your mind will end, and you will be well. This knowledge is superior to all knowledge, sacred, and can be easily put into practice. This is called the "Path of Devotion." O Arjun! I am present everywhere in this world. All beings reside in me, but I do not reside in them. Although I am the cause of their origin and their maintenance, yet I am not in them. Being in ignorance, they do not recognize me, because they do not have devotion for me. The easiest way to practice devotion is to keep faith which dispels ignorance. From the seeds of faith itself, the plant of belief starts flourishing, and then the flowers of devotion blossom on this plant.

Shri Krishna says: O Arjun! Like the wind, I am present everywhere. All things reside in me. I am the creator of the world, the one who maintains it, and the destroyer of all. At the end of the cycle of the ages (Satyug, Treta, Dwapar, and Kaliyug), at the time of the holocaust, all things end and merge into Me. When the second cycle begins, I create them again with my power. The whole world is under me. It is created again and again by my will and finally destroyed by my will. The ignorant do not know me, the Lord of the world, because they are surrounded by illusion. But the wise who recognize my truth worship me with the desire to take refuge in me. Some worship me with my single form (Nirakar or formless) and some with my many forms (Sakar or corporeal) in their mind. O Arjun! All of them are my devotees.

Lord Krishna explains further: O Arjun! I am all-pervading. Understand in this way: I am the resolution of the yajna; I am the yajna; I am the support of the ancestors; I am the plant of the yajna; I am the mantra, the ghee, the fire, and the oblation. I am the father, mother, shelter, and grandfather of this universe. I am Omkar. I am also Rik, Sama, and Yajurveda. I am the maintainer, the master, the refuge, and the well-wisher. I give heat, stop and bring rains. I am immortality, and also death itself. Soul and matter (real and unreal) both are in me.

The Lord says: O Arjun! Of all the creatures in the whole world, man is the only creature who has a conscience and who knows good and bad. No other creature has this power. The accounting of sins and virtues, that is, destiny, is made only for humans. That's why according to one's destiny, after enduring sins and virtues, a person has to be born again in the human form. Humans go to heaven (Devlok) according to the virtues they have accumulated. After enjoying the heavenly world, when their virtue is over, they return from heaven and take birth in the human form to work again. In this way, they are always trapped in the cycles of life and death.

Lord says: O Arjun! Different people in the world worship different gods. The reality is that they all actually worship me. All the gods and goddesses are parts of me. I am the only enjoyer and master of all the sacrifices. People worship different deities while keeping their desire for enjoyment and worldly pleasures. Its gains are only momentary. The fruit is certain, but it is perishable, gets destroyed quickly after use. They again get trapped in the cycles of life and death. Therefore, O Arjun! Those who worship the gods take birth among the gods, those who worship the ancestors go to the ancestors, those who worship ghosts take birth amongst them, and those who worship me they all unite with me.

Arjun asks: O Madhusudan! By creating an illusory world, you have created countless attractions to mislead man at every step. To help a person who has lost his way, what do you want from him? Do you want offerings of gold and silver? Do you want tasty and clean dishes from your devotee?

The Lord clarifies: O Kaunteya! I want nothing from a man but reverence. I don't ask for anything else. He should not make big offerings to me. I don't want offerings of gold-silver, ghee-sandalwood, dishes etc. With reverence and devotion, even a fruit, a flower, a leaf of a flower, a drop of water, or half a grain of rice, I accept this type of offerings with more happiness than the devotion of the devotee. Even if this is not possible, even a tear of devotion is okay, I accept that too. In a tear soaked in reverence, my whole personality blossoms. The tears of devotion or repentance, even if shed at the last moment after having committed millions of sins, I accept that unique offering as well. By washing away all the sins of a man with those tears, I make him sinless like a newly born baby. I do his welfare; I give him freedom (salvation).

The Lord further explained: Hey Arjun! A man should do the work but should not be attached to the fruits. There is an easy way to do this — **"To dedicate the work itself to the Lord."** Therefore, O Arjun! Whatever you do, whatever you eat, whatever you donate, and whatever austerity you perform, do it as an offering to me. I accept it. In this way, you will be free from the bondage of karma and attachment to the fruits. Thereafter, the responsibility of all your good and bad results will be mine.

O Arjun! No one is small or big, high or low for me. I am equal to all living beings. Everyone is equally entitled to get my abode. The righteous, the wicked all have the right to worship. Due to the effect of prayers, even a miscreant becomes righteous quickly.

That's why, O Arjun! Always engage your mind in thinking of me, become my devotee. You will surely find me.

CHAPTER-10

VIBHUTI YOGA (DIVINE GLORIES)

Preface:

From the seventh to the ninth chapters of the Gita, Lord Krishna has described His forms, features, and looks at many places. Placing these looks in the heart, one can easily meditate upon Him. The Lord is an ocean of virtues. To understand the full extent and the powers of His forms is not under the capabilities of ordinary human intelligence. That's why it becomes necessary that some examples are given, so that the grandeur of God's features can be depicted. Wherever in this world, whenever this magnificence is seen, we will bow down to it with respect and remember the Supreme Soul. In this chapter, these Vibhutis, i.e., magnificent features of the Lord, are described.

Summary:

Lord Krishna says: O Arjun! For the benefit of the devotees, I am illustrating my forms and features once again. Listen carefully.

Even the gods and sages do not know my origin. Because I myself am the cause of their origin and of all others. The person who recognizes me as unborn and eternal, the darkness of his ignorance gets dispelled, and he becomes free from sins.

The Lord explains further: Hey Arjun! I am the Lord of all. Just as the living beings are born from me, similarly, their different feelings, such as forgiveness, truth, happiness, sorrow, birth and death, fear and fearlessness, etc. are also born from me. Seven Maharishi, Manu, etc. who created the universe are also born from me. I am the origin of everything. The whole creation is run by me. Those who recognize these qualities and power of mine, worshiping me and mediating on me enable them to live happily. And they finally find me.

Then Arjun asks: O Vasudev! You are the Parambrahma, the Supreme abode, you are the Holy. It is you who has said that sages, etc. worship you in the form of Aadidev, unborn and God. O Lord! O Father! No one knows your true form; only you know yourself. You tell me about the personalities of your form and also suggest how I can recognize you while contemplating you.

Lord Krishna replied: O Arjun! The expanse of my various forms and looks is endless. Let me tell you some of their special features. I am the soul sitting in the heart of all living beings. I am their origin, their middle, and their end. Among Adityas I am Vishnu, among bright things I am the Sun, among vayus I am Mareechi, among nakshatras I am the Moon, among Vedas I am Samaveda, among devas I am Indra, among senses I am the Mind, among beings I am the Consciousness, among Rudra I am Shankar, among yakshas I am Kubera, among demons I am Prahalad, among priests I am Brihaspati, among sages I am Bhrigu, among weapons I am Vajra, among animals I am the Lion, among birds I am Garuda, and among those who deceive I am the Gambler. Whatever happens in this world, it all happens according to my will; nothing can happen without my will. Good and bad also happen only when I let it happen. Knowing this, a man should leave ego and avoid evil, because I am also the provider of good and bad. You should understand that this whole world is based only on a fraction of my Vibhuti.

Lord's Cosmic Form

CHAPTER-11

VISHWAROOP DARSHAN YOGA (LORD'S COSMIC FORM)

Preface:

At the end of the 10th chapter, the Lord concluded by saying that the entire universe is held in a fraction of his form. Hearing which, Arjun had a deep desire to see that great form. In this chapter, at Arjun's request, Lord Krishna has shown His Virat Roop (the Great Form). Virat Roop has been described and praised in most part of this chapter. That is why this chapter is named Vishwaroopa Darshan Yoga. There is also a mention of Sanjay, a major character of the Mahabharata. Sanjaya has got divine vision by the grace of Maharishi Veda Vyas. He is narrating to Maharaj Dhritarashtra the running commentary of the battle field. Sanjaya begins the description of that wonderful moment when the Lord appeared in His divine form.

Summary:

Arjun says: O Vasudeva! Because of the ultimate secret you have shared with me regarding the soul, my mind's ignorance and delusion have ended. Yes, God! You have illuminated me with your light. However, the brightness of your light could not end all my desires. Even now there is a desire left in me, which has not died.

Lord Krishna asks: O Arjun! What is such a desire, which even the brightness of my light could not kill?

Arjun: Of your darshan (to see you in real).

Krishna: You are seeing me in person.

Arjun says: No, God! I want to see your real complete form. I have heard in detail about your different qualities and your different forms. You have taken different forms in different incarnations as well. I want to see all those forms and all the qualities, together, at the same time. O Lord of the whole world! If you are pleased with me, then fulfil this last wish of mine.

Lord Krishna says: O Partha! I have always called you my friend. I can definitely fulfil your wish. But your eyes will not be able to bear the glare of the sight of my great form. O Arjun! The capacity of your vision is not big enough to accommodate my entire divine form.

Arjun says: The scope of my vision is small, but your compassion, your mercy is not small. As the donor does not change his mind and reduces his donation after finding that the beggar's bag is small, in the same way, O Lord! Give me that divine vision so that I can see your great form.

God says: O Arjun! Like a true devotee, you have defeated God today. It's a good thing. I will definitely fulfil your wish. Today, because of you, all the gods and goddesses will also be delighted to see my rare form. First I give you that vision, which can see this great form.

On the other side in the palace, Sanjaya is listening to the dialogue between Krishna and Arjun on the battlefield. Describing this wonderful moment, he says to Dhritarashtra: Maharaj! Saying thus to Arjun, Yogeshwar Krishna revealed his supreme and great form, giving Arjun divine vision. Sanjay further says: O Maharaj! It seems as if crores of suns have descended on the land of Kurukshetra. The huge form of God has spread out from Patal to Prithvi Lok and from Prithvi Lok to Swarg Lok. All creations have become alert to see this divine universal form of God. Arjun is saying something to the Lord, amazed and thrilled.

Arjun says: O Mammoth Figure! O Mighty Form! Oh God! Seeing your huge figure, I am amazed, and scared. From heaven to hades, your huge and fearful form is visible. You are beyond the limits of my divine vision. Where does your existence begin and where does it end, I am not able to understand anything. I see, all the sons of Dhritarashtra with their assisting kings and Bhishma, Drona, Karna, and our chief warriors are also entering your dreadful mouth for destruction. I am confused. Please tell me, who are you?

O Great-Armed! Your fiery light is heating the whole world with its brilliance. Have mercy on me. Tell me who are you in this fierce form?

Lord Krishna (in the huge form) said: O Arjun! Gracious to you on your request, I have made you see the eternal and infinite form in my supreme glory, with the effect of my yogic power. This huge form that you are seeing, I haven't shown this to anyone before. I have shown this divine form only to you out of affection. You should not be worried. O son of Pandava! Look at me. I am Mahakal, the destroyer of all worlds. You see,

Drona, Bhishma, Karna, and other brave warriors have already been killed by me. You are just an instrument to kill them in the battle. In my mouth, every moment, thousands of universes keep getting merged. And millions of universes keep emerging from my mouth. All these creations made up of crores of stars and lakhs of suns function only based on my will. I create them whenever I want; I liquidate them when I want. I am the birth; I am the death. O devotee! The form that I have assumed at this time because of your devotion and prayer is complete only in your own thinking and understanding. You can neither understand my existence with your intelligence, nor can you see my complete form with divine vision. All your imaginations will fail to see my entire existence. Yes, only with devotion can you feel my vastness, just a feeling. Therefore hold this divine form in your heart with full faith and devotion. Remember my name and let go of any fear and anxiety.

Confused and horrified, Arjun prays: Oh God! Hey Trilokinath! You are right. My eyes will not be able to tolerate the brightness of your great form. Seeing this huge and formidable form of yours, my mind is racing with panic and anxiety. You have given me divine vision to see your great form, but these eyes do not have enough tolerance and even this much capacity to see your most brilliant form at a long stretch. That's why O Vishwanath! Oh God! I pray to you again to rid my nervousness and anxiety, Lord! Show me your cool form. I want to calm my mind by seeing your quadrilateral form. Once again, wearing conch, chakra, Padma, mace, please show me the darshan (sight) in your gentle four-armed form.

Lord Krishna (in the gigantic form) says - O devotee! I had already told you that you will not be able to tolerate the glory of my great form. Still, just to respect you, I have assumed this gigantic form, and now I accept your second prayer as well. According to your wish, I take a quadrilateral form.

Arjun says: O Janardan! Seeing your great form, my mind was terrified. Seeing your four-armed form, my heart has become calm and my mind stable.

Krishna says: O Arjun! You are the most fortunate that you have seen both my great form and my four-armed form. This vision of mine is rare even to the gods. This darshan (sight) can be had only by pure devotion. One who dedicates all his actions to me, remembers me alone, becomes my devotee, gives up attachment to lusts, and loves all beings, he finds me.

BHAKTI YOGA (DEVOTION TO GOD)

Preface:

In the previous chapters, the Lord has, at various places, praised the worship of the nirguna-nirakar (formless) and the saguna-sakar (corporeal) forms of God. Arjun himself is a devotee of Lord Krishna in his sagun-sakar form. Arjun wants to clarify his position regarding which is better between the formless and the corporeal paths. In this chapter, the Lord has clarified the difference between the formless and corporeal forms of God. Due to the much importance of worship of the corporeal God, the manifestation of devotion, the description of its means, and the characteristics of the devotees have been explained in this chapter. That's why this chapter is named Bhakti Yoga.

Summary:

Arjun says: O Vasudeva! When you show me your divine form, you also say that this great form is not complete. It is complete only for my own understanding. It means that in reality you are so huge, so gigantic that you cannot have any shape.

Krishna says: Yes, Arjun! This is the truth. I am eternal, infinity, have always been and will always be. In all creations, there is no such place, no location, where I do not exist. That's why I have no shape; I am formless.

Arjun says: God! You have also said that you are in the elephant; you are in the cow, and you are also in the ant.

Shri Krishna says: Yes, this is also true.

Arjun says: God! Then, in this way, you are also corporeal.

Shri Krishna says: Yes, Arjun! As I am standing like this, in front of you, in a human avatar (incarnation), this is also my corporeal form. Apart from this, I have also shown you the incarnations that I have taken in the past. All of these are corporeal. But my true, and the vastest form, is formless.

Arjun says: O Lord! So, it has been proved that you are incorporeal as well as corporeal. Your devotees, who consider you to be real, worship you by making idols of your incarnations. And the devotees who consider you formless, they worship you in formless form. Which of the following is correct? Those who worship your idols, or those who worship your incorporeal form?

Shri Krishna explains: O Arjun! No one is wrong. My devotees worship me in any form, corporeal or formless, in fact, they all worship me and me alone. Everyone meditates only on me in their mind. Even by making idols of my incarnations, worship is done. Those who do not see my huge form in idols, they worship my endless and eternal formless form. Both types of devotees, walking on the path of devotion, move toward my supreme abode, and find me.

Shri Krishna further says: O Arjun! **For the common man, the formless form remains a problem for meditation. In fact, no one can properly contemplate the formless form of the Supreme Truth. The formless form is beyond human imagination. That's why most of the human beings, knowingly or unknowingly, are devotees of the corporeal form. It is the easiest to worship my corporeal form.**

O Arjun! My devotees are very unique and peculiar. Some consider me as their father and establish a son's relationship with me, whereas some consider me as their mother. Some consider me as a friend, whereas some establish a relationship of love with me. Like the gopis of Gokul, who forget all the customs of the world in my love, My feature stays in their eyes, in their mind, at all times, everywhere. I reward the devotees for their devotion in the form they want. I am their father, as well as mother, as well as friend, and son as well.

Arjun asks: O God! Can a devotee even love you?

Lord Krishna says: O Partha! Love is devotion. One who does not have love in his heart, how can he be my devotee? In truth, love is God.

Arjun says: O Krishna! There is no method to love someone, but there are many methods to worship. Your devotees worship you according to these so many methods.

Lord Krishna explains: Hey Arjun! Worship is the meditation of the mind, and what does the meditation of the mind have to do with rituals and methods? As two lovers love with their hearts, so it goes with devotion. People have created these rituals and methods for their own convenience. I also accept the worship of those who worship by those rituals and methods. But **I do not see whether my devotee is worshiping according**

to the rituals or not. I see only the spirit and feelings of the worshipper. I only see whether he has love and devotion toward me or not. I do not accept that worship in which there are only rituals and methods, but there is no love and devotion.

Describing the methods of devotion, Lord Krishna says: O Arjun! Different devotees adopt different means to worship me. Some keep my corporeal form in their mind and dedicate all their actions to me. Some try to reach me by controlling their mind through meditation, asana, and yoga. There are some who, renouncing the fruits of their actions, continue to do whatever is in their capacity. Whatever may be the way, with continuous effort, the color (influence) of devotion starts rising, and the joy of being close to God starts.

Describing the various characteristics of a devotee, Lord Krishna says: O Arjun! My devotee remains equal in happiness, sorrow, fear, etc. He does not have any desire for lust; he is pure; he is efficient; he stays away from the attractions of the worldly pleasures; being determined, he has equanimity in both auspicious and inauspicious results. He has neither a friend nor an enemy. He remains the same in both respect and dishonor. Being content with whatever he gets and by being silent, he wanders like a loner and remains equanimous in all situations. In this way, one who remains faithful is my devotee.

CHAPTER-13

KSHETRA KSHETRAJNA VIBHAG YOGA (NATURE, SOUL, AND THE DIVINE)

Preface:

In this chapter, Lord Krishna has explained the difference between the bodies, the master of the body, i.e., the soul, and the master of all, i.e., the Almighty, the master of the whole universe. In this chapter, kshetra means the body, and kshetrajna means the one who resides in the body, its master, i.e., the soul. God is the master of all, controlling innumerable bodies and souls. The universe moves according to His instructions. Soul has also been called jeeavatma at some places. The words soul and jeevatma are synonyms. After knowing the clear difference between all the three (i.e., body, soul, and the Divine), man understands the reality of life. He renounces worldly pleasures and starts trying to concentrate his mind on God.

Summary:

Arjun says: O Madhusudan! I want to know what is worth knowing about body, nature, soul, God, and knowledge, and what the relationship between all of them is. Please tell me about all these things.

Lord Krishna says: O Arjun! There are three things in this world. One is this body; the second is the soul living in this body, and the third is the one who is present everywhere, the Supreme Soul, the Lord of the whole universe. The one who lives in the body in the form of soul never dies, and the body does not last forever. The soul leaves one body and assumes another, just like a man putting on new clothes after taking off his old clothes. The soul is a part of the Supreme Soul, but it knows and is limited only to its specific body in which it resides. God is the creator of all the bodies and all the souls that reside in them, as well as the entire universe. God is present everywhere, and everything moves at his behest.

Hey, Arjun! Let me tell you about the construction of the body and the substances used in the making. First of all, earth, water, fire, air, and sky are the five great elements. Then there is ego, intelligence, and the three gunas (sattva, rajas, tamas). After this, the five sensory organs — eyes, nose, ears, tongue, and skin. Then there are the five organs of action — speech, feet, hands, anus, and reproductive organ. Then above these senses, there is the mind which is in a subtle form within the body. In this way, there are total eleven senses including the mind. Then there are five subjects of these senses — smell, taste, shape or look, touch, and sound. In this way the body is formed from the group of these twenty four elements. When the life force (consciousness) flows in this body, then desire, hatred, happiness, sorrow, and patience are generated in it. These have been called villainy because they make human beings dance at their tunes. The whole body made up of twenty four elements and seven villainies is called Karma kshetra (field of action). This body is a temporary material object made up of nature. It is subject to the laws of nature. There are six types of changes in the body. It takes birth, grows, persists, produces offspring, decays, and finally dies.

Hey Arjun! Every soul has its own individual domain. The body in which the soul resides has to bear the consequences of its deeds. The body moves according to the laws of nature. The soul is definitely the master of the body, but it has no control over nature. The senses are so strong that they are always eager for gratification. Under the influence of material desires, the soul is enamored of this illusory world. That's why it keeps on adopting one body after another. Sometimes, the soul has to take birth in the form of a deity, sometimes an animal, sometimes an aquatic animal, sometimes a bedbug, and sometimes a human. Due to its ignorance, it remains trapped in the cycles of life and death, undergoing various pleasures and pains. Nature repeatedly brings him to the material world and keeps on giving him an opportunity to enter the heavenly world again and again by doing good deeds. The ultimate goal of the soul is to become one with the Supreme Soul. Having a clear knowledge of God, the soul engages in the service of God with love and devotion and gradually attains salvation by uniting with God. Salvation or Moksha means getting rid of the repeated cycles of life and death.

Lord Krishna further says: O Arjun! Let me tell you what

the meaning of knowledge is. I am giving important information about how unity with God can be achieved with the help of knowledge. O son of Kunti! Humility, non-violence, simplicity, purity, absence of arrogance; realization of the flaws of birth, death, old age, and diseases; affection with natural objects like children, wife, and home; performing selfless duty; treating happiness and sorrow with equanimity; to have exclusive love and devotion for God; all this is called knowledge, and whatever is beyond this is ignorance. O Arjun! God is present everywhere. He is eternal and infinite. The whole universe moves at his behest, arises from him and merges into him when the time comes. God alone creates, sustains, and destroys. It is the God who makes the senses perform wonderful functions.

Hey, Arjun! The Lord and His illusion, both are continuous since time immemorial. Illusion means Maya. Maya, which keeps on dancing over nature, gives rise to disorders and many bad deeds. It is because of Maya that the man experiences happiness and sorrow, sin and virtue. It is an absolute truth that without the inspiration of God, nothing in this world can even move. Therefore, O Arjun! Knowledge is to understand that the creature who has fallen into this world due to chance should understand his position and reality of life. Understanding the distinction between the body, the soul, and the Super soul, having unremitting devotion and love for the Lord, he should try to become free from this material world and become one with the Lord.

GUNA TRAYA VIBHAG YOGA (THREE QUALITIES OF NATURE)

Preface:

In this chapter, Lord Krishna tells Arjun about the three qualities of nature, i.e., sattva, rajas, and tamas. The temperament of man is formed due to these three qualities of nature, and then on the basis of the temperament, different tendencies and attitudes develop. The Lord has explained the nature of these three gunas (qualities), their functions, cause and power, how, in what condition they bind the soul, and how by overcoming them, man can reach near the Almighty; all such aspects have been clarified.

Summary:

Arjun says: O Krishna! You have said that in order to become 'Sthitprajna' (stable), keep the mind stable just like the light of a lamp remains stable in a vacuum. That is, don't let the mind wander here and there. This means that while doing work, keep the mind under the control of the intellect rather than controlling the mind, isn't it?

Lord Krishna says: No, Arjun, there is danger in trusting the intellect also because "when one's doom approaches, one's mind, one's intelligence works perversely." That is, when the adverse time comes, the intellect of a man takes him on the wrong path.

Arjun says: O Madhusudan! Man should neither act according to his will, nor follow the advice of the intellect, then what should the poor man do? In such a situation, how would one lead a life against one's instincts? O Lord! Show me some way how a man can change his tendency and adopt the path of liberation and salvation.

Lord Krishna says: O Partha! Before changing the tendency, it is necessary to know how the tendency is formed. This knowledge is far more superior than all the wisdom mentioned so far. Hey Kuntinandan! In all the species, all the living beings that are born and bear bodies, nature is the mother of all, and I am the father who sows the seed. O Arjun! A man is born with the three gunas of sattva, rajas, and tamas with him since birth. The universe has been created on the basis of these three qualities. All the three qualities are present in all the living beings. But inside every living being, one or the other of these three qualities is predominant. The quality which is more dominant, the character of that person is dictacted accordingly. Rajogun-dominant man has a longing for opulence, pomp, and royalty. The one with Tamogun is lazy and careless, wherein negative emotions like malice, anger are filled completely.

Arjun: And the one with Sattva guna?

Krishna says: Sattva guna is the best quality. A person with Sattvic qualities is straight and truthful. By the way, in the nature of every human being, all the three qualities are present in some or the other quantity. But a man's character is determinted by the quality which is predominant. Whatever one's attitude is, so is one's taste. So every human being works according to his temperament, attitude, and taste.

Arjun asks: O Krishna! Can a man, by changing these tendencies, improve and go toward higher qualities?

Krishna says: Yes, Arjun! Between the three Gunas, there is a constant competition to remain dominant. Man, in comparison to other living beings, is more intelligent and prudent. If one takes a resolution, he can develop good qualities through practice. He can defeat Rajogun and Tamogun.

Arjun says: O Madhusudan! What happens after the death of the people living in these qualities?

Lord Krishna explains: Hey Partha! If a man dies when Satgun is high, he goes to the pure worlds of Maharishis (saints). When the Rajoguna is dominant, the person who dies takes birth in a human form. When the mode of Tamoguna increases, the dying man takes birth in the animal form.

Arjun says: O Lord! What is the conduct of a person who has conquered these three qualities? What are his symptoms? How can one go beyond all the three modes of nature?

Yogeshwar Krishna explains: O Partha! The man who is satisfied with what he has got, does not desire more, acts according to his merits, whose mind is stable, who treats pleasure and pain equally, for whom iron, stone, or gold are equal, for whom the dear and the unloved ones all are equal, on whom there is no effect of praise or censure, for whom honor and dishonor are alike, one who is equanimous to friend and foe, such a person is said to have conquered all the three gunas. That means he cannot be distracted by these qualities. O Arjun! Without action, without attitude, one cannot even breathe. Therefore, man is bound to perform actions. The person who wants to go beyond these qualities, he should dedicate all his deeds to me and do not desire for the fruits. By doing so, his karma (actions) does not become an obstacle in the way of his success, because I am Brahma; I am Moksha; I am Sanatan Dharma, and I am Eternal Happiness. Such a person attains ultimate happiness by uniting with the Supreme Soul.

MANAGEMENT CONCEPTS:

Verse: 14.5

Verse: Sattvam Rajastam Iti Gunah Prakriti Sambhavah |
Nibadhnanti Mahabaho Dehe Dehinamavyayam || 5 ||

Meaning: O Arjun! Nature is made up of three qualities: Sattva, Raja, and Tama. As soon as the living being takes birth, he also becomes bound by these three modes of nature. He works under the influence of the magical powers of these three qualities.

Lord Krishna says that the personality of a man is formed as a result of the association of the three qualities of nature: Sattva, Raja, and Tama.

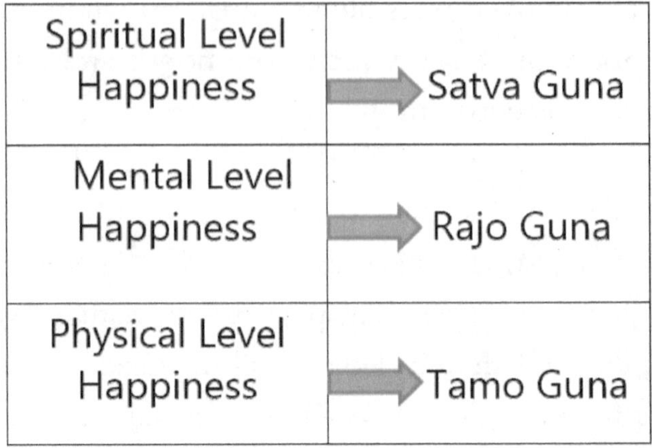

Tamo guna is at the lowest level; above that is Rajo guna, and Sattva guna is at the top and considered the best. Tamo guna makes a man ignorant, prone to illusion, running after the pleasures of the senses, egoistic, lazy, and careless. A person with Rajo guna is full of boundless aspirations and cravings, works for Sakam Karma, have longings for status, prestige, and dominance. A person with Satva guna is more knowledgeable, prudent, improved in living, away from the attractions of enjoyment and luxury, and keeps on doing good deeds without any desire for the fruits. Although all the three qualities are present inside a human being, one or the other of these three qualities is more prominent. The quality which has more dominance, the character of the man is formed accordingly.

Being knowledgeable and prudent, if a man wishes, he can rise from the lower level of qualities to the higher levels with practice. In all human beings, the basic feeling of going to a higher level is hidden. This happens only when he starts getting the taste and the delight of a higher level of quality. In this way, a man can develop sattva guna while moving upward.

Much has been written in the field of management about leadership styles and qualities. It is widely accepted that a good leader should have the quality of "Handling people appropriately and effectively." The Stanford Research Institute, California has determined the importance of understanding and handling people appropriately as a management strategy as follows:

Importance	**Strategy**
12%	**Knowledge**
88%	**Handling People Appropriately**

It is necessary for a successful leader that first he should understand the nature of the people, only then he can handle them effectively. This very nature of man (Sattva, Raj, and Tama Gunas) has been explained thousands of years ago by Lord Krishna in the Bhagavad Gita. All the concepts and theories that have been developed in sociology and modern management on the nature of man and the art of "handling people" are based on the knowledge of the Bhagavad Gita.

Graham Maslow, an American sociologist, in his 1954 book "Motivation and Personality," proposed five core human needs as the basis of human behavior and motivation. This theory later came to be popularly known as "Maslow's Hierarchy of Needs." The Hierarchy of Needs is a psychological idea and is particularly useful as an assessment tool in sociological research, management training, and higher education. This theory has a wide impact and is accepted globally, because it explains things in a very simple and understandable manner. Most people are quick to recognize these needs in their own and others' personalities.

Maslow's Hierarchy of Needs framework is shown below.

Self-actualization
Esteem needs
Belongingness and love needs
Safety needs
Physiological needs

Maslow's Hierarchy of Needs

Maslow suggested that individual needs can be viewed as a pyramid, with the largest and most basic needs at the bottom, and the more motivating ones at the top. According to this principle, until a person does not achieve the first stage, he does not move forward to achieve the second stage. That is, only after the attainment of the first step, he's inspired to make various efforts to achieve the second step. All needs are met in an orderly manner. According to this principle, a person moves from the lower level to the higher level.

1. <u>Physiological Needs</u>: According to Maslow, the primary need of man is his physical satisfaction. Physical needs include food, water, clothing, sleep for the rest of the body, etc. After these immediate needs are met, it moves to the next stage.

2. <u>Safety Needs</u>: Once the physiological needs are satisfied, the safety needs take priority and dominate the human nature. These needs are health, personal security, financial security, etc.

3. <u>Need for Love and Belongingness</u>: The third level of human

needs is interpersonal and involves feelings of belongingness. Human beings need to love others and be loved by others. These needs are family, friendship, sense of trust, small social relationships, etc.

4. <u>Esteem needs</u>: After the need for love and belongingness is satisfied, he feels the need for self-respect, to live a dignified life in the society. For this, he tries to make a different identity from others, that is, to show himself as special. Because of which all the people of the society should treat him with love and respect.

5. <u>Self-actualization</u>: Maslow has considered self-actualization to be the best for a human being. At this level the person gets to know his inner powers and gets inner satisfaction. Self-actualization means knowing the soul. Recognizing worldly bitterness and truth is self-actualization. It signifies the highest level of completeness of human conscience. If you look at the history of the world, only a few great men have achieved this level. For example, Gautam Buddha, Guru Nanak, Mahatma Gandhi, Jesus Christ, Swami Vivekananda, Prophet Mohammad, Lord Mahaveer, Abraham Lincoln etc. They have left a lasting impact on mankind and continue to exercise positive and inspiring influence on the minds of people.

So far we have seen that Lord Krishna has told that the three gunas born of nature —Sattva, Rajas, and Tama—are present in all human beings. Whichever quality is more dominant, the character of a man is determined accordingly. The basic feeling of going to a higher level is hidden in all human beings. Some people reach the level of Sattva Guna by self-motivation, but most people reach that height by taking inspiration from family or society. Maslow's hierarchy of needs is made up of five levels. It is based on the three qualities of nature as described in the Bhagavad Gita. This is shown below.

Maslow's Hierarchy of Needs   **The Three Gunas (Qualities of Nature)**

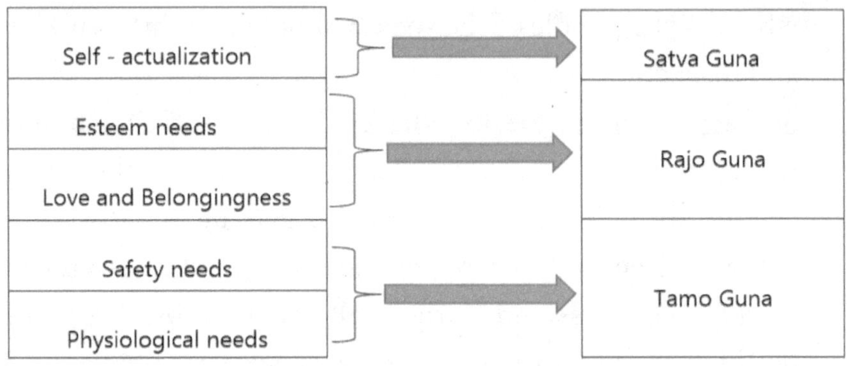

The wisdom of the Bhagavad Gita is always relevant in every country and in every age. The welfare of man and nature is possible only with the knowledge of Gita.

PURUSHOTTAM YOGA (STRUCTURE OF THE ILLUSORY MAYA WORLD)

Preface:

In this chapter, the Lord explains to Arjun about the structure of the world and its creation by taking the example of the ficus tree (peepal tree). It has also been explained that there are three types of characters in this world. One is this body which is perishable; the other is the soul, the master of this body, which is immortal, which keeps moving in the cycles of birth and death, constantly adopting one body after another while intermingling with the material world. Apart from these two characters, above them there is a third super character, i.e., the Super soul, the Almighty who nurtures all and provides them with the facilities of enjoyment according to their deeds. He is the all-powerful, omnipresent God, who is also called Purushottam.

World – Tree

Summary:

Arjun says: O Krishna! You have said that this world has arisen from You, You are its nurturer and You are its destroyer. This whole creation is a game of your illusion. Hey Keshav! What is the form of this world of Maya?

Lord Krishna says: O Partha! If you look carefully with your wisdom, you will see that this world of Maya is like an inverted ficus tree, with its roots at the top and the branches and leaves at the bottom. See this through your inner eyes, Arjun.

Arjun says: O Keshav! I can see this world-tree. Its roots are above and have come out of You.

Lord Krishna says: Yes, Arjun! As I said, this world of illusion (Maya) has arisen from me. That's why its roots are in me, and the place of Maya, because it is below me, is why this tree is upside down.

Lord Krishna says: O Arjun! Being the creator and expander of this world, Brahma is the main branch of this tree, and Vedas are its leaves. O Partha! Taste, touch, look, smell, and sound — these five are in the form of twigs of the branches of this tree. O Partha! This Maya tree is nurtured with the waters of the three gunas, i.e., sat, rajas, and tamas. A man who is stricken with lust and attachment remains entangled in the branches of this tree. O Partha! This tree is eternal, infinite. This tree is a symbol of the illusion of the world.

Arjun says: O Madhusudan! When this tree is the creation, then its huge shadow must also be spread out everywhere. So how can a man escape from its shadow?

Shri Krishna says: O Arjun! It is okay that this tree is large, but its creator is even larger than this. Hey, Arjun! When you will cut this tree with the sword of wisdom and asceticism, you will see God. He is omnipresent and pervades all.

Therefore, O Partha! You come to my shelter.

Arjun says: O Madhusudan! You have said that after death, the soul has to go to heaven, etc. to enjoy happiness, or to hell, etc. to experience sorrow. This means that the soul does not have happiness and sorrow only on the earth but also it has to suffer happiness or sorrow in heaven or hell.

Lord Krishna says: No, Arjun! Happiness and sorrow cannot touch the soul anywhere, at any place, or even at any time. Because the soul is the light form of me, the imperishable God.

Hey Arjun! I am not under Maya, but Maya is under me. And happiness and sorrow are the creation of Maya. When Maya cannot take me in its circle, how can the happiness or sorrow created by Maya touch me? Happiness and sorrow are only the enjoyment of the body, not of the soul.

Arjun says: O Keshav! It seems that you are misleading me in the illusory words. Accepted that happiness and sorrow are only the enjoyment of the body, the soul is detached from them. This body, which suffers them, dies. That body does not go ahead. Then who goes to heaven or hell to experience happiness and sorrow?

Lord Krishna says: Jeevatma.

Arjun says: Jeevatma?

Krishna says: Yes, Partha! The Jeevatma.

Arjun asks: What is the Jeevatma, Keshav?

Lord Krishna says: Look! When someone dies, in reality, only this gross body outside dies. The subtle body inside the gross body does not die. That subtle body, carrying the light of the soul with it, leaves this mortal world and goes to other worlds. That same subtle body is called the Jeevatma

Arjun says: It means, when the soul leaves a body, it takes the jeevatma along with it.

Lord Krishna explains: No, Arjun! This explanation is not so simple. See, a drop of water inside an ocean is not separate from the ocean; it is a part of the same ocean. That drop does not automatically go out of the ocean. Yes, if someone takes that drop of water in a vessel, it looks different from the ocean. Similarly, the Jeevatma in the form of a subtle body keeps a piece of that Light of the soul inside itself and takes it with it. This is the journey of the soul, which keeps on moving from one body to another until it is united with the Supreme Soul.

Hey Arjun! Just as the wind carries the smell with it from one place to another, in the same way, when the jeevatma leaves a body, it takes along its previous body's instincts, its sanskars, the account of its good and bad deeds, i.e., its destiny.

Arjun asks: O Madhusudan! Is there any such place from where one does not have to come back, and this cycle of life and death ends?

Lord Shri Krishna says: O Arjun! As I mentioned earlier, there are three types of characters in this world. One — this body which is perishable. Second — the master of this body, the soul which is immortal, and third — the master of both of them, i.e., the Almighty, Immortal God, who is called Purushottam. O Arjun! The brightness of the sun that illuminates the world, the radiance of the moon, it all comes from me. I reside in the heart of everyone. Wise men can understand the difference between the body, the soul, and the Supreme Soul, and move toward salvation by worshiping me without attachment.

O Arjun! The place where the cycle of birth and death ends is the Supreme Abode. That means my abode, where no one has to come back from after reaching. This is called Moksha.

DEVASURSAMPADVIBHAG YOGA (DIVINE AND DEMONIC NATURE)

Preface:

In the previous chapters, the Lord has said: "The fools who have the demonic and monstrous nature do not worship me but despise me. On the other hand, people with divine nature considering me as eternal and imperishable constantly worship me with love." Naturally, a curiosity builds to know the characteristics of human beings with divine nature and those of demonic nature. In this chapter, the Lord has described in detail the characteristics and nature of both.

Summary:

Lord Krishna says: O Arjun! In this world, there are two types of nature of human beings. One like the deities and the other like the demons. When there is an excess of divine qualities or divine tendencies, human nature is like that of gods, and when there is excess of demonic qualities or demonic tendencies, human nature is like that of demons. <u>There are only these two castes of humans in the universe, no matter wherever they are born, whatever they are called.</u>

O Arjun! **The first qualification in the characteristics of a man with divine nature is fearlessness.** Then clean-heartedness, constantly striving for knowledge, charitableness, self-restraint, philanthropy, study of the scriptures, austerity, simplicity, non-violence, living with the truth, restraining anger, renunciation, peace, caring for others, not finding fault, showing kindness to all living beings, not being greedy, soft in mind, feeling ashamed of doing wrong, not being distracted or depressed in any endeavor, protecting the weak, forgiving, having patience, not being jealous, avoiding the desire for respect and honour — all these are the signs of a man of divine nature.

O Partha! In humans with demonic nature, arrogance, pride, vanity, anger, harshness, and ignorance are seen.

O Partha! Divine qualities lead a man to salvation, and demonic qualities keep him in the cycles of continuous birth and death. O Arjun! You should not worry because you are born with divine qualities.

Thereafter, Lord Krishna elaborates a little about the demonic qualities: O Arjun! Those who are demonic, they do not know what should be done and what should not be done. Neither purity, nor proper conduct, nor truth is found in them. They say that this world is false, baseless, and it is not controlled by God. They say that it arises from the relationship between man and woman, and there is no other reason than lust. The actions of such people are terrible; their mind is dull; they hold on to their evil thoughts, and all their tendencies are toward the destruction of the world. There is no end to their wishes. They live in ego and false pride. There is no limit to their worries. They want new enjoyment every day. They keep building castles in the air. They do not differentiate between justice and injustice while collecting money for the nourishment of their desires.

Hey Arjun! A demonic person thinks: Today I got this and tomorrow I will get that; today I will kill this enemy then I will kill another; I am strong; I am the master of all, who is like me; I will perform yajna for fame and popularity; I will give charity and enjoy different types of pleasures. Believing such in his mind, he remains happy, and in the end gets trapped in the delusion and gets hell. Hey Arjun! Those who are envious and cruel, who hate God, I leave them in the cycles of life and death by continuously putting them in different demonic births.

Arjun says: O Madhusudan! The senses are very powerful. They pull you toward sensual pleasures. An innocent person can get trapped in their strong powers and become of demonic nature. There must be some way to save this poor man from the demonic qualities. O Keshav! Show me a way by which one can be saved from demonic tendencies.

Shri Krishna says: Yes, Arjun! There is a way to avoid demonic tendencies. There are three gates to hell from demonic tendencies — lust, anger, and greed. A person should give up these, because they lead to the downfall of the soul. O son of Kunti! The person who escapes from these three gates of hell does charitable work and thus gradually moves toward the Supreme Abode.

Hey Arjun! In order to make human life successful, a man should keep on doing his duty without any desire, keeping prudence in what to do and what not to do according to the laws made in the scriptures, i.e., as per morals.

CHAPTER-17

SHRADDHA TRAYA VIBHAG YOGA (THREE KINDS OF FAITH)

Preface:

At the end of the last chapter, the Lord has given the instruction to perform actions according to the scriptures. Not everyone has the knowledge of the scriptures. Therefore, in this chapter, the Lord has thrown light on devotion (faith), because it is the devotion that reveals the true nature and attitude of a person. In this chapter, all types of devotion, i.e., Satvik, Rajasi, and Tamasik are discussed. Due to its effect, the different symptoms that are seen in all the activities of a person like food, charity, penance, etc. have been described in detail. In the end, a special explanation of Om Tat Sat has been presented, which has come for the first time in the verses of Gita.

Summary:

Arjun says: O Krishna! In many situations, people do not know or understand the rules and regulations of the scriptures, yet they continue to worship the deities according to their imagination with love and devotion. What would be their position in such a case? They get success or does their devotion go in vain?

Lord Shri Krishna says: O Arjun! Devotion is that straight and simple path which leads a man toward love and peace. Hey Arjun! I have already told you that a human being is born with the three gunas of sattva, rajas, and tamas. Inside every living being, one out of these three qualities is predominant, and man's character depends on the quality which is predominant. In this triple gunas creation, there are three types of faith in man — sattvic, rajasi, and tamasi. That's why, according to their respective beliefs, those with sattva guna worship deities, those with rajo guna worship Yaksha, Gandharva etc., and people with tamo guna worship ghosts and spirits.

Hey Arjun! According to the different qualities of nature, there are differences in food, sacrifice, penance, and charity. They are not all alike. All of them also have three types.

Hey Arjun! The diet which increases longevity, purity of mind, strength, health, happiness, and interest is called Satvik. That which is pungent, sour, spicy, and hot is Rajas, and eating this causes sorrows and diseases. The food which is half-cooked, tasteless, stale, foul-smelling, false, and impure in other ways is dear to Tamasi people.

Hey Arjun! The Yajna which is performed without any desire for fruits, which is performed with full devotion considering it a natural duty, is considered to be Satvik. A yajna in which there is expectation of fruits and arrogance is considered rajas, and a yajna in which there is no method, no yield, no mantra, and no renunciation is tamas.

Describing the differences of penance, Lord Krishna says: O

Arjun! In which there is respect for saints; there is purity; there is observance of celibacy, and there is non-violence is called physical penance. Speech which is truthful; loving and beneficial; not hurting anyone; chanting Vedas—this is the penance of speech. Happiness of mind, gentleness, contemplativeness, restraint, and pure feeling—this is called mental penance. The three types of physical, speech, and mental penance done with utmost devotion, without any desire for the fruits, are called Satvik penance. The penance which is done arrogantly for respect, hospitality, and show is called Rajasi. It is neither permanent nor eternal. The austerity that is done because of foolishness, obstinately, by suffering, and to destroy or cause pain to others is said to be Tamasi penance.

Lord Krishna says the following about charity: O Arjun! The charity which is given considering it a duty, without the expectation of any reciprocation, at the right time and place, and to a deserving person is considered Satvik. But the charity in which there is hope of return, and in which there is hesitation, is called Rajasi. And the charity which is given without hospitality in an unholy place, at an inappropriate time, to an unworthy person is called Tamasi.

Thereafter, Yogeshwar Krishna told the form of 'Om Tat Sat' and said that these names are the reminder of God. Lord Krishna says: O Arjun! Since the beginning of creation, these three words Om Tat Sat have been used to indicate Parabrahma. That's why a man should always start all the activities like Yajna, charity, and penance by chanting Om. Om means monosyllabic Brahma. Tat means that and Sat means Truth, the form of welfare. Meaning that — **God is one, He is, He is the truth, and He is the benefactor.** The faith of those who perform

Yajna, etc. without any desire for the fruit is Satvik. If he does something different from the scriptures because of not knowing it or even knowing it, he is still considered innocent.

O Arjun! The action done without dedicating it to God is considered without faith. It is called 'asat' (false), and it is wasted both in this life and in the next lives.

MOKSHA SANYAS YOGA (EPILOGUE)

Preface:

This is the last chapter of the Bhagavad Gita. In fact, the Gita ends in chapter 17 itself. The eighteenth chapter is a supplementary summary of the subjects explained in the previous chapters. That is, the summary of all the teachings has been given clearly so that there is no doubt. After contemplating the previous chapters, doubts remain in Arjun's mind, because the sanyas of the Gita seems to him to be different from the prevalent sanyas. He thinks renunciation (tyag) and retirement (sanyas) are two different things. Clearing this doubt of Arjun's, the Lord has given the essence of Gita-Knowledge in this last chapter.

Summary:

Arjun says: O Lord! I want to know the difference between and nature of tyag (renunciation) and sanyas (retirement).

Lord Krishna said: O Partha! tyag (renunciation) and sanyas

(retirement) are based on man's deeds. Deeds (Karma) are mainly of three types. For the fulfilment of material desires, man creates many enterprises. Such actions which are performed for the fulfilment of material desires or wishes are called actions performed for the sake of desires or Kamya-karma. Second, there are necessary and natural actions, such as breathing, eating, drinking, sleeping, wearing covering, etc. to protect the body. The third karma is called "Paramarthika," i.e., philanthropy, which is done for the welfare of others. Of these, O Arjun! Renunciation of actions based on material desires, i.e., "Kamya-karmas," is the sanyasa of the Gita, and renunciation of all the fruits of actions is the tyag of the Gita.

Hey Arjun! Karma done for the sake of charity, such as Yajna, charity, and penance, should never be abandoned. All these activities should be performed without any kind of attachment or expectations of result.

Hey Arjun! There are three types of renunciation. According to the nature and circumstances, the proper deeds like penance, war, agriculture, business, service, etc. are called prescribed deeds or Niyat-karma. Renunciation of prescribed actions under ignorance, frustration, or delusion is called Tamasi-tyag. Renunciation of prescribed actions due to fear of the pain of the body is Rajas-tyag. When a man performs the prescribed actions considering it his duty and gives up desires for all material fruits, i.e., in a selfless manner, then his renunciation is called Satvik-tyag.

Arjun asks: O Keshav! How is renunciation of karma possible for a man who is under the control of your mighty illusion? This way he can never attain salvation. Will there be some way to get it?

God says: Yes, Arjun! Undoubtedly, it is impossible for any living being to give up all actions. For this, O Arjun! A man should keep on doing his work but should not be attached to the fruits of his work, i.e., work in a selfless manner. **So instead of relinquishing action, one should go on relinquishing the attachment.** In this way, he will slowly start moving toward salvation and will be able to escape the cycles of life and death. The good, bad, or mixed results of a man's deeds get accumulated in the form of destiny, and after death he definitely gets it back in the next birth. But a person, who renounces the fruits of his actions, or in other words, works selflessly, does not have to experience the pleasures and pains of the fruits of his actions in any birth.

Arjun asks: O Lord! Every action has some or the other result. Then how is it possible that one does not have to experience the pleasures and pains of the fruits of action?

God explains: O Parth! To understand this fact, let me give you the example of Sankhya philosophy. Hey, Arjun! There are five reasons for success of any action: The place of action, i.e., the body; the doer of action, i.e., the soul present inside the body; the instruments of action, i.e., the senses; various efforts for actions, and lastly, the God, on whose command all activities take place. God is the ultimate power behind all the activities. Hey, Arjun! An ignorant person does not understand that God is within him as a friend and is directing his actions. Although the place, the doer, the efforts, and the senses are material causes, the final and prime cause is the Lord Himself. One who does not see the Lord out of arrogance considers himself to be the chief doer. But a person who sees and believes in the Supreme Lord as the chief Director, while doing work, is never deluded and is able to accomplish everything, and at the same time, is free from the arrogance of being the doer. Such a person never has to suffer the pleasures and pains of the fruits of his actions.

The Lord says: O Partha! To do the daily work, first the inspiration arises and then the action takes place. Inspiration has three components — Jnaata (the knower), Jnan (the knowledge), and the Jnaeya (knowable). Similarly, there are three components for the completion of action — the senses (the instruments of action), the action itself, and the doer. The one who decides the goal of the duty is called the Jnaata (knower). The attitude with which we decide the goal is Jnaan (knowledge). The goal to be fixed, i.e., the target of knowledge, is called the Jnaeya (worth to know). When there is inspiration, the doer comes to the fore. Thereafter, with the help of the senses in which the mind is involved, the real work is accomplished.

God says: O Arjun! I have said earlier that the universe has been created on the basis of three gunas—Sattva, Rajas, and Tama. All the three gunas (qualities) are present in all the living beings in this world. According to these three qualities of nature, there are three different forms of knowledge, action, and doer. The knowledge with which a person sees the same soul in every living being, whether it is a deity, a human being, an animal, a bird, or a water creature, is called Satvik knowledge. The soul living in everybody is imperishable and is a part of the Almighty. From this point of view all creatures are equal. Whatever difference is seen is due to assuming different bodies. The knowledge through which we can see the spirit of God in every living being, i.e., even though everything is different, when we go deeper and find everyone to be the same, that is Satvik knowledge.

O Arjun! The belief that the physical body is the living entity, and that when the body is destroyed, the living entity is also destroyed, is Rajasi knowledge. According to them the body is the soul, and beyond this there is no special soul or God. All these concepts are generated from Rajoguna.

O Arjun! The knowledge of an ordinary man is always Tamasik. The person who does not acquire knowledge through various means, his knowledge remains limited only to the body; he is called a normal human being. Such knowledge has no relation with the Supreme Truth. It is very similar to the knowledge of ordinary animals, such as the knowledge of eating, drinking, sleeping, protecting, etc. The knowledge that keeps only the body happy in every way is called Tamasi.

The Lord says: O Arjun! Like the department of knowledge, there are departments of action as well. Where there is no desire for the fruits, there is no ego and attachment—that action is Satvik-karma. Where there is a desire for enjoyment, where "I do" is the ego, and where there is commotion from it—that is Rajas-karma. Where there is no concern for the result, loss, violence, or power and that which is done under the control of lust and attachments—that is Tamas-karma.

God again says: O Arjun! Like the action, the doer should also be understood to be of three types.

A Satvik doer is one who does his work without ego, with determination and enthusiasm, and remains composed in its success or failure. The doer who, being attached, wants to enjoy the fruits of action, and the one who is greedy, jealous, impure, and distracted by pleasures and pains, is called Rajasi. The doer who is materialistic, obstinate, deceitful, and adept at insulting others, and who is lazy, always sullen, and likes to delay work is called Tamasi.

The Lord says: O Arjun! I describe the different types of intelligence, firmness of mind, and happiness according to the three modes of nature.

O Arjun! That intelligence is Satvik by which man knows what should be done and what should not be done, which work he should be afraid of and which work should be done with courage. What binds and what liberates. The intelligence that tells the difference between good and bad is Satvik. The intelligence, which cannot differentiate between morality and immorality, good and bad, is Rajasi. Those who always work in the opposite direction from the direction in which they should work consider truth as untruth and untruth as truth, and accept those religions which are not religion in reality; their intellect is called Tamasi.

O Arjun! The person who is capable of concentrating his mind on the Supreme Soul while keeping the activities of the mind and senses under control, his determination is Satvik. He does not get distracted by any other work. The determination of a person who is desirous of the fruits of action in religious or economic pursuits, whose only desire is the gratification of the senses, whose mind, life, and senses revolve around gratification, is said to be Rajasi. The determination, which does not allow a man to give up condemnation, fear, grief, oversleeping, despair, enjoyment, intoxication etc., is called Tamasi.

O Arjun! I am going to tell you about three types of happiness according to the three qualities of nature. In order to see God by peering into the soul, controlling the mind and senses, one has to follow various rules and regulations. All these methods are very difficult and in the beginning seem bitter like poison. But when one succeeds in following these rules, then God is definitely visible to him. He starts tasting the real elixir and attains the happiness of life. Thus, that which appears like poison in the beginning but gives happiness like nectar in the end is called Satvik happiness. Sense-enjoyment which seems sweet in the beginning but later becomes like poison is Rajasi happiness. That happiness, which is blind to the Supreme Lord, which is alluring from beginning to end, and which arises from condemnation, laziness, and delusion, is called Tamasi.

O Arjun! In this world, among the demigods in the heavenly worlds, no one exists who is free from these three modes of nature.

Hey Arjun! In this way everything can be divided into three parts. The four varnas (Brahmin, etc.) have also come into being due to having more or less of these three qualities. There should be peace-loving, self-restraint, penance, purity, forgiveness, simplicity, and righteousness in the work of a Brahmin. Kshatriyas should have bravery, strength, determination, patience in battle, generosity, and leadership skills. Farming, cow protection, and trade are the duties of a Vaishya. And the duty of a Shudra is labor and service to others.

O Arjun! While doing one's own duty one becomes devoted to God. Actions performed with the spirit of serving God lead a man toward Him. That's why a man should go on doing work in harmony with his natural temperament. No action is small if it is done with the spirit of service to the Supreme Lord. For example, even when there is smoke with fire, fire has always been considered pure. Similarly, even if there are some shortcomings, work born of natural temperament is considered appropriate.

For example, a butcher takes care of his family by slaughtering animals and selling their meat. Slaughter of animals by him is not wrong; for this work he is not called sinful because he has got this work according to nature-born qualities. Hey, Arjun! Duties derived from nature-born qualities are performed without the desire for the fruits, that's why there is no sin for such actions.

The Lord says: O Partha! True renunciation means that a man should always consider himself as a part of God, and think that since he is a part of God, the fruits of his work should be enjoyed by God. Having thus controlled the mind, he does not become attracted to the objects of sense-gratification. Such a person is solitary, eats little food, and is equal among other human beings. He relinquishes ego, lust, anger, etc. He always remains focused on God. That knowledgeable yogi becomes eligible to attain God.

O Arjun! A true devotee can feel and understand the transcendental qualities and forms of God as they are because of his pure devotion. One can understand the Lord by devotion and enter His abode along with his personality. The attainment of God by way of renunciation, i.e., worshipping God as formless form either by Sankhya yoga or by Jnana yoga, is like the rivers that meet the ocean. Rivers cease to exist after merging with the ocean. But the devotee worshipping God as corporeal form maintains his existence in the same way as an aquatic creature in the ocean. O Arjun! My pure devotee attains the imperishable abode by my grace even after being engaged in all kinds of activities under my protection.

Overwhelmed with emotions, Arjun says: O Keshav! You have destroyed the darkness of ignorance by kindling the light

Take refuge in Krishna

of knowledge in my mind. The veil of attachment and all illusion has been lifted from my mind. Freed from all bondages, I offer myself at your holy feet. Order me what to do now.

The Lord Krishna says: O Arjun! Now you go ahead to fulfil your duty in the battlefield. Pick up your bow, Gandeev, pull its string, and declare war.

The Bhagavad Gita ends here after Arjun surrenders to the Almighty. After this point, Sanjay speaks the last five verses. Sanjay says: By the grace of Maharishi Veda Vyas, I heard the sermon spoken by Lord Krishna to Arjun. I have also seen the wonderful gigantic form of Lord Shri Krishna and am rejoicing again and again remembering it. I believe that wherever Yogeshwar Krishna and the archer Arjun remain, Victory, Glory, Super powers, and Morality will surely reside there. The final commandment of the Gita is the essence of all religions and ethics — **"You worship Lord Krishna and go to His shelter."** This is the essence of the eighteenth chapter.

MANAGEMENT CONCEPTS:

Verses: 18.63, 18.72, and 18.73

Verse: Iti Te Gyanmakhyatam Guhyadguhyataram Maya |
Vimrishyaitdasheshen Yathechhasi Tatha Kuru || 63 ||

Meaning: Lord Krishna says to Arjun, "Thus I have told you this most secret knowledge. Think about it completely, do as you want, and move forward."

Verse: Kacchidatechchutam Partha Tvayikagren Chetsa |
Kachchidgyansanmoh Pranashtaste Dhananjay || 72 ||

Meaning: Hey Partha! Have you listened carefully to this knowledge with a concentrated mind? And Hey, Dhananjay! Have your ignorance and delusion been destroyed?

Verse: Nastho Mohah Smritirlabdha Tvatprasadaanmayachyut |
Isthitosmi Gatsandeha Karishye Vachanam tav || 73 ||

Meaning: Arjun said, O Krishna! O Lord! Now my attachment is gone. By your grace, my memory has come back. Now I am free from doubts and determined and ready to act according to your orders.

In the Bhagavad Gita, Lord Shri Krishna has preached all the ways a person can improve the quality of his life and achieve his goals successfully. Lord Krishna tells Arjun that I have told you all the wisdom of Gita, think about it, and do whatever you want in future. I never interfere in the freedom of the living being. Lord Krishna was teaching Arjun like a guru (teacher), so he asks Arjun whether he has understood the Bhagavad Gita correctly or not. If you have not understood, then I am ready to narrate a particular part or the entire Bhagavad Gita again.

Now it is Arjun's turn to tell how the knowledge of the Bhagavad Gita has impressed him. Did he come out of the darkness of ignorance or not? Arjun says: O Lord! After listening to the wisdom of the Bhagavad Gita from you, I have become free from all illusions. I also understood that you are not only my friend but also The Almighty. I surrender before you. I am ready to go for battle as per your orders.

In the context of management, Lord Krishna has used different leadership styles in different situations to impart the wisdom of the Bhagavad Gita. Every teacher, after imparting knowledge, is eager to know how much his disciple has learned and understood. Similarly, after giving complete knowledge of the Bhagavad Gita, Lord Krishna wants to know from Arjun how much he has learned and whether he has become capable or not (this is given in the verse 18.72).

Companies and organizations regularly organize training and development programs for their employees. After the training is over, they see how much the employees have learned. They also measure the impact of this training on the company's output. From the management angle this is known as "Return on Investment." The Return on Investment or ROI of Gita teachings is explained by Arjun in verse no. 18.73. Arjun has learned and understood the Gita completely.

After imparting complete knowledge of the Bhagavad Gita, Lord Krishna makes Arjun free to take decisions on his own, and inspires him thus: Arjun! Proceed according to your thoughts. This is stated in verse no 18.63. In the management context, it is called "Delegation." Now the time has come when Arjun has learned and become capable of taking further responsibilities. This is what happens in industrial areas. After imparting training, the employees are put to work by giving them responsibilities.

Verses: 18.74, 18.75, 18.76, 18.77, and 18.78

Verse: Ityaham Vasudevasya Parthasya Cha Mahatmanah |
Samwaadmimamshraushamadbhutam Romaharshanam || 74 ||

Meaning: Sanjaya said: Thus I heard the talks of both the great beings Lord Krishna and Arjun. This knowledge is so wonderful that my body is thrilled.

Verse: Vyasaprasadachhutavanetadguhyamaham Param |
Yogam Yogeshwaratkrishnaatsakshatakathayatah Swayam || 75 ||

Meaning: By the grace of Vyasa ji, I personally heard these most secret words spoken by Yogeshwar Krishna to Arjun.

Verse: Rajansamsmritya Samsmritya Samvadmimamadbhutam |
Keshavarjunyoh Punyam Hrishyami Ch Muhurmuhuha || 76 ||

Meaning: Hey, Rajan! When I remember again and again this wonderful and holy conversation between Lord Krishna and Arjun, I am overwhelmed with ecstasy every time.

Verse: Taccha Samsmritya Samsmritya
Roopamatyadbhutam Hareh |
Vismayo Me Mahan Rajan Hrishyami Ch Punah Punah ||77||

Meaning: Hey, Rajan! I am more and more amazed, and rejoice again and again, when I remember the wonderful divine form of Lord Krishna.

Verse: Yatra Yogeshvarah Krishno Yatra Partho Dhanurdharah |
Tatra Shrirvijayo Bhutirdhruva Neetirmatirmam ||78||

Meaning: Where there is Lord Krishna and where there is Arjun, the supreme archer, there certainly resides opulence, victory, superhuman strength, and ethics. This is my opinion.

It is to be understood that, just as Arjun was fortunate to see and hear Lord Krishna directly, similarly, by the grace of Maharishi Veda Vyasa, Sanjaya was also able to see and hear Lord Krishna with the help of divine vision. Like Arjun, Sanjaya also heard the entire Bhagavad Gita and saw the divine form of Lord Krishna. Sanjaya says: "I am the witness of those words, of those dialogues that took place between Lord Shri Krishna and Arjun. And remembering Lord Krishna's wonderful gigantic form, I am amazed and delighted. I have seen great events happening in the world. The flow of this wonderful knowledge will last for ages. By the grace of Vyas ji, I became a witness to this great event."

In the last verse of Bhagavad Gita, Sanjaya lists four benefits of reading Bhagavad Gita and applying it in life. Sanjay says: Where there is Lord Krishna and the archer Arjun, that is, where the Bhagavad Gita is present and read, there will always be four benefits.

1. Opulence: There will never be any shortage of money.
2. Victory: He will always be victorious wherever he goes.
3. Super Power: Even the weakest man becomes a lion after reading the Gita.
4. Ethics: The person who will follow Bhagavad Gita in his life, he will become an honest man with character, morals, principles, and values (i.e., he will understand the difference between right and wrong).

If we consider the context of management, then this part of Gita is known as Feedback part. In these last five verses, Sanjaya is giving feedback on the entire Bhagavad Gita.

Feedback is an important principle of management and is the final part of the management process. Feedback control is a technique used in the workplace. Feedback gives us strength to improve if we are not on the right track. It informs the managers about the difference between what the employees are actually doing as compared to what is expected. This technique helps managers to identify problem areas and address them.

An example of feedback: if a person wants to pick up an object such as a book, the brain commands the hand to reach for the book, and the eyes continuously send feedback to the brain as to where the hand is relative to the book.

In the end, to express my gratitude to the Bhagavad Gita, I am quoting these beautiful lines of Dr. Vivek Bindra, world renowned management expert and great motivator and speaker.

You have served in my plate more than I can afford;
No matter how many difficulties come, I have faith in you.
What I got was the grace of God,
And what I lost was my ignorance.

- Dr. Vivek Bindra

"The Bhagavad Gita is the king of all scriptures."

BIBLIOGRAPHY

1. Jaidayal Goyandaka (Samvat 2066): Shrimad Bhagavad Gita - Tatva Vivechani, Gita Press Gorakhpur.

2. Sudhanshu Ji Maharaj (2018): Shrimad Bhagavad Gita - Geetamrit Pravachan, Vishwa Jagriti Mission, Delhi.

3. Bhaktivedanta Swami Prabhupada (1995): Srimad Bhagavad Gita Yatharoop, Bhaktivedanta Book Trust, Bombay.

4. Mahatma Gandhi (2020): Gita-Mata, Prabhat Paper Backs, New Delhi.

5. Sanskrit Sahitya Prakashan (2010): Shrimad Bhagwat Mahapuran, Vishwa Vijay Pvt. Ltd., New Delhi.

6. Swami Adagadanand (2004): Yatharth Gita, Shri Paramhans Swami Adagadanand Ji Ashram Trust, Mumbai.

7. Lokmanya Bal Gangadhar Tilak (2020): Shrimad Bhagavad Gita, Rashtriya Hindi Sahitya Parishad, World Literature India, Gemini Printing Service, New Delhi.

8. Dr. Ram Shankar Tiwari (2014): Shrimad Bhagavad Gita ke 18 adhyayon ki Sahaj Evam Saral Vyakhya, Pustak Mahal, New Delhi.

9. Shiv Khera (2011): You Can Win, Macmillan Publishers, New Delhi.

10. Roopa Pai (2015): The Gita for Children, Hachette Book Publishing, Gurgaon.

11. Vinod Malhotra (2013): Gita me Management Sutra, Prabhat Paper Backs, New Delhi.

12. Er. Srinath Arcot and Dr. Balachander Arcot (2015): Bhagavath Gita - Man Management, Manimekalai Prasuram, Chennai.

13. Swami Vivekananda (2019): Bhagavad Gita as Viewed by Swami Vivekananda, Advaita Ashram, Kolkata.

14. The 7 Habits of Highly Effective People (2020): Stephen R. Covey, Simon & Schuster UK Ltd., London.

15. Swami Vivekananda (2021): Geeta Aur Krishna, Rashtriya Hindi Sahitya Parishad, World Literature India, Gemini Printing Service, Delhi.

16. Dr. (Mrs.) Sudha Pandey (2003): Kathopanishad Tatha Srimad Bhagavad Gita ka Tulnatmak Adhyayan, Amrit Prakashan, Varanasi.

17. Strategic Management (1991): Indira Gandhi National Open University, Madhav Book Binding House, Delhi.

18. Managing Men (1988): Indira Gandhi National Open University, Rajbandhu Industrial Co, New Delhi.

19. Management Functions and Behaviour (1988): Indira Gandhi National Open University, Allied Publishers Pvt. Ltd, New Delhi.

ABOUT THE AUTHOR

Mr. Diwakar Mishra is an engineering graduate, 1978 electrical batch from MNR Engineering College Allahabad (now known as MNNIT Allahabad), and MBA with 36 years of diverse industrial experience in private and public sector companies. He has proven credentials in various managerial positions in the domain of manufacturing, commercial, human resource management, and project execution. He firmly believes that the knowledge of Gita is capable of bringing fundamental change in human thought process. Drawing from his life and professional experience, this book is his humble attempt to bring the insights of Gita to the masses with a fresh and simple approach.